Dare To Struggle! Dare To Win! A Personal Memoir

BY
KHALID RAHEEM

ABSTRACT:

This book is a collection of my memoirs and analysis of several groups, organizations, initiatives and movements that I have been a part of from the early 1980's throughout the first decade of the 21st century. My participation and involvement was varied. In some instances, I played a strictly supportive role: in other situations, my role was more strategic, tactical and decisive.

I'm writing these memoirs in the hope of sharing perspectives that will be both informative and instructive for activists and organizers today, particularly those who embrace, embody and represent the Black radical tradition and the Black revolutionary class. My personal political development has not been upwardly linear. There have been peaks and valleys, highs and lows. However, my desire for freedom and justice has been consistent and my willingness to strive for such has remained undaunted.

The book is divided into three broad chronological sections and several subsections (chapters) which focus on particular groups and initiatives of that decade. I have been blessed and fortunate to have met many educators, activists and organizers throughout my life and appreciate the time and energy needed to combat the various expressions of white-supremacy and economic injustice we continue to experience. This story is their story as well.

Most importantly, this is the story of the countless individuals, families and communities impacted by decades and generations of systemic oppression and their collective struggles to survive it and hopefully to defeat it.

FOREWORD:

I want to personally acknowledge and thank Dr. Anthony Mitchell of Penn State University, who several years ago, suggested that I write this type of book. My apologies to Brother Tony for taking so long to get here. I would also like to acknowledge the members and supporters of the New Afrikan Independence Party for inspiring me (twisting my arm) again to put pen to paper in service to the community. Special thanks to Brian, Doug, Lisa, Zuri, Emma, Cathy, Shandre and Ramona.

Blacks/New Afrikans today face a serious impasse. We have witnessed the failures of liberal democracy in addressing the plight of Black people, especially the working-class and poor. We have also witnessed the corresponding rise and escalation in white-supremacist violence from private formations (such as vigilantes, neo-Nazis, white-nationalists) and the state (such as the police and the criminal justice systems). Various political pundits attribute the emergence of this situation to the politics of Donald Trump, while others, (me included) see it as no more than just a variation of white-supremacist political economy.

Trump is not an aberration, but rather a different version. He represents the literal confluence of corporatism, the military, the police, white-nationalism and electoral politics: early 21st century U. S. styled fascism. We must continue to be organized, militant, vigilant and flexible in order to defeat it.

Table of Contents:

National Black Independent Political Party (NBIPP)..................................page 1

Pittsburghers Against Apartheid...................................page 8

Islamic Confederation of North America... page 10

Jesse Jackson Presidential Campaigns: (1984 & 1988) ....page 15

African American United Front (AAUF)................................page 18

Campaign for a New Tomorrow..............................page 23

Community Mosque, Inc................page 25

Gang Peace Council of Western PA: (GPC)....................................page 38

National Council for Urban Peace & Justice (NCUPJ)..................................page 61

Million Man March Local Mobilization Committee & the Million Man March...................................page 72

Justice for Jonny E. Gammage.......page 80

October 22nd Coalition...............................page 89

Jericho '98......................................page 93

It's About Time, BPP...............................…......page 100

NAABPP............................page 105

Honorable Mentions..............................page 107

Closing Comments............................page111

PART 1

1981-1990

- **National Black Independent Political Party (NBIPP)**

- **Pittsburghers Against Apartheid**

- **Islamic Confederation of North America**

- **Jesse Jackson Presidential Campaigns (1984, 1988)**

CHAPTER 1

The National Black Independent Political Party (NBIPP):

I was released from prison in the summer of 1981 after serving more than ten years. I am originally from Philadelphia but during the course of my incarceration, I was transferred to the state correctional institution in Pittsburgh. Why was I incarcerated and how did I wind up in southwestern Pennsylvania? Well, that's a whole other conversation. Needless to say, in the summer of 1981, I hit the streets running.

While in prison, there were a group of us who took college courses offered by both Community College of Allegheny County and the University of Pittsburgh. Two of our professors were Curtis Porter and Rob Penny from the University of Pittsburgh's' Black or Africana Studies Department.

Some of us had been friends, associates (or rivals) on the streets as well. A few had come from backgrounds as radicals, revolutionaries and activist on the streets and/or within the prisons. We often had very spirited debates and discussions regarding U.S. politics, culture, international affairs and criminal justice reform. Sounds odd to some, I'm sure. Prisoners were very politically aware, even those who had engaged in some of the most counterproductive and self-destructive behaviors imaginable. We had trouble managing and overcoming various addictions and challenges: but, we were not stupid, numb or oblivious to the social climate in which we lived.

Sometime in 1980, a group of prisoners including Marshall Calloway, Rodney 'Kamau' Jackson, and myself had a discussion regarding an article we read concerning an initiative to create an independent Black political party. The article contained information about either an upcoming or previously held founding convention in Philadelphia. We were excited about the idea and prospect for such an organization. Within our larger group, many of us had read, studied and debated the writings of Manning Marable as well as the euphoria and disappointments emanating from the historic National Black Political Convention held in Gary, Indiana in 1972. As early as 1980, we understood how crucially important it was for Black people to break the hegemony of the democratic party and chart an authentic agenda and course for Black freedom and liberation.

As we reviewed the proposed platform and program for this new political party, we noticed that a plank specifically addressing the issues and challenges of prisoners was absent. In those days, the term 'mass incarceration' was not yet in popular use, but we wanted to convey to the leadership and framers of the document that it would be an oversight not to include specific language and demands regarding the plight and situation of Black prisoners. So after meeting and drafting a letter of concern with recommendations, we met on the yard: ratified our letter of concern and promptly mailed it to the leadership of the National Black Independent Political Party (NBIPP).

Shortly afterwards, we received a response from the NBIPP. Much to our surprise, not only did the NBIPP agree to incorporate our recommendations as part of the national platform, they actually invited us upon release to join the leadership cadre of the National Black Independent Political Party. They wanted to know if there were any members within our group who would be released shortly and who would be willing and able to serve and work in building the NBIPP. I think Marshall was released from prison before me, perhaps by a few weeks or months.

As I stated previously, I was released from prison in the summer of 1981. This is how I came to be a member and leadership cadre of the National Black Independent Political Party (NBIPP). Ron Daniels, one of the co-chairs of NBIPP had roots and ties to the Pittsburgh area which certainly accounted for the strong Pittsburgh representation within the party.

I came to meet several Pittsburgh area activists and organizers through our membership and participation with NBIPP, many of whom would remain associates, friends and comrades for life: people like Rick Adams, Gail Austin, Fred Logan, Saladin Howze, and Malik Bankston. Others such as Aisha White and Carl Redwood, I met previously through their work around prison reform and advocacy for prisoners' rights.

I came to appreciate the brilliance and dedication of folks like Ron Daniels and Barbara Sizemore up close through working with them and experiencing the challenges of developing an independent political formation that centered the experiences of Black people. Having been fresh out of prison, the NBIPP provided Marshall and I with numerous opportunities to travel, network and learn about the people and conditions outside of southwestern Pennsylvania. We had a lot of catching up to do in terms of understanding the real social, cultural and economic climate existing throughout urban Black America in the early 1980's.

These were the lean years during and immediately after the collapse of the steel industry, notably U.S. Steel and other such companies. The Pittsburgh region was severely impacted with layoffs, bankruptcies and foreclosures. Other areas of the United States were hit hard as well. We traveled to places like Detroit, Chicago, Baltimore and Youngstown, Ohio.

I recall the bleakness and lack of economic vitality, for example, in downtown Youngstown. Empty sidewalks on a Saturday afternoon. Closed storefronts with 'for rent' or 'for sale' signs in just about every other window: department stores with so few shoppers that you could literally look through the front window and see straight through out the back!

In Chicago, a few of us ended up buying breakfast for a group of young boys who came into the restaurant we were attending asking for something to eat. They were some of the hardest and most desperate looking children I had ever seen in my life. I'm sure they probably became ripe recruits for whatever gangs were in the area, not because of some sort of genetic criminal predisposition, but due to economic hardship and abandonment.

Detroit provided me with my first experience with a 'no contact' sales exchange. We went to a chicken and fish type of store, ordered some food which we purchased and received behind a bullet-proof glass window. Put your money down, spin to us on the tray: when food is ready, we spin it back. No touch, no contact. I later found out that this type of security procedure was in response to all the robberies that had taken place throughout the area.

I don't recall exactly what Marshalls' legal status was during this period, but I was still on parole. My original parole was to the eastern side of Pittsburgh (Homewood) and I reported to an office in East Liberty. My parole officer was a middle aged white woman who was supportive, flexible and not over-bearing. I complied in all the areas required, except travel. In those years, for the most part, I traveled at will. I found the whole process of requesting permission, checking in with destination authorities and carrying around a letter or something to be a bit too authoritarian. Today, I would not suggest that any one on parole or probation follow my example. It was reckless and immature. If you must travel, follow the process. Stay out of prison.

Anyway, Marshall and I traveled just about everywhere with the party: learning, networking and contributing in any way we could. However, there was definitely one exception: Grenada. The NBIPP had scheduled a gathering in the Caribbean nation of Grenada during the administration of revolutionary leader and comrade Maurice Bishop. We both laughed out loud about how it might be just a little too difficult trying to explain to a parole officer or anyone else that we were late reporting back because we somehow got stuck in Grenada. So, ultimately we declined to attend. Unfortunately, a few years later Maurice Bishop was betrayed, overthrown and assassinated in what many of us believe was a coup backed and supported by the United States and its CIA operatives.

In my opinion, the National Black Independent Political Party was a great idea and concept that never came into tangible fruition because of several factors, most notably ideological struggle (debate, discussion) over what was to be the prevailing or dominant political line of the party. I contend that most of this struggle was not essentially driven by firm adherence to ideological purity on behalf of its proponents, but rather personality conflict.

There were endless meetings and debates about what people should believe, very little about what the community should actually be doing and how to get it done. There were major schisms regarding the role of NBIPP members who also were members of other organizations with particular political lines, for example the Socialist Workers Party (SWP) and the Congress of Afrikan People (CAP). I think we even had some NBIPP folks still claiming allegiance to the democrats! Controversies also arose about the role and prominence of Marxist-Leninism, Maoism, Revolutionary Nationalism, Cultural Nationalism, etc. It appeared that several folks were attempting to dominate the ideological direction of the NBIPP or perhaps hijack the entire organization in pursuit of some other agenda, yet to be determined. We spent more time reviewing and revising documents and position papers than we did actually working with and organizing the Black community.

The party appeared to be dominated by Black/New Afrikan intelligentsia who had become drunk from their academic prowess and achievements. In a span of just a few years, the party went from at least a couple thousand representatives (those who attended the 1980 founding convention in Philadelphia) to probably less than 100 people. To the best of my recollection, we never organized any independent NBIPP political campaigns or presented any candidates for electoral office. We failed to materialize as a viable independent Black political alternative to either mainstream political party (Democrats, Republicans).

I have often reflected on my experiences with NBIPP and the lessons learned. For example, ideological dogmatism is non-productive when attempting to organize an independent political party that engages in mass-based electoral political struggle (running candidates for political office). Also, party leadership cannot include persons who are still clinging to either the republican or democratic parties, or those who maintain leadership (strategic, tactical) positions in other organizations that are in hostile competition with the party. It can only breed and facilitate opportunism, distrust and contempt.

However, I continue to salute those sisters and brothers who attempted to break the yoke of the Democratic Party stranglehold on the Black psyche and liberate Black political capital (for example, votes and endorsements).

CHAPTER 2

Pittsburghers Against Apartheid:

Many of the same people involved with the Pittsburgh chapter of NBIPP were also members of the advocacy group Pittsburghers Against Apartheid (PAA). However, PAA also included many who were part of the traditional civil rights crowd (NAACP, Urban League), but who were firmly opposed to apartheid. Charles Kindle of the Penn Hills branch of the NAACP was one of those types: an inspirational leader, orator and organizer.

The group was already actively engaged when I became involved in the early 1980's shortly after my release from prison. We were part of a growing local, national and international movement to dismantle the apartheid regime of South Africa and demanded the release of all its political prisoners, most notably, Nelson Mandela.

Calls for divestment from the South African economy were gaining popularity within the United States and internationally. Here in Pittsburgh, we waged an ongoing campaign to halt the trade and distribution of the South African 'Krugerrand', the apartheid regimes premier gold currency. The Krugerrand was heavily marketed and sold throughout the United States. One of the brokerage firms doing marketing and sales was a company named A.G. Edwards. I remember participating in the several days of protest and demonstrations targeting various offices throughout the area, particularly the office located in downtown Pittsburgh on Smithfield Street. Dozens of us were chanting, marching in synch in front of their office, urging people to not buy the Krugerrand and demanding an end to apartheid in South Africa.

At some point, the police showed up and a mild, but escalating verbal confrontation started. They threatened some with arrest if we didn't discontinue, but we ignored them. The police were attempting to intimidate the protesters and had not anticipated much resistance. Eventually, cooler heads prevailed and we finished what we had started. Pittsburghers Against Apartheid is an example of the important linkage between local, national and international movements for justice and freedom. Unfortunately, in places like Soweto and Pittsburgh, economic apartheid (Jim Crow) still exists for the majority of working class and low-income Black people.

CHAPTER 3

Islamic Confederation of North America:

As a Muslim I was an active member of the First Muslim Mosque of Pittsburgh, arguably one of the oldest and first Black or African-American originated masjid or mosque within the United States. Imam Mansur who led the masjid had regularly provided guidance and support to the incarcerated orthodox or Sunni Muslim community throughout the Pittsburgh area. Along with another brother named Muhammad Ali, they helped to develop and establish a strong linkage between the outside community and those of us on the inside. They gave us counsel, education, leadership and examples on how to function and operate as Muslim within the larger context of a profoundly racist and oppressive environment that hated us for being Black and resented us even more for embracing Islam. May Allah be pleased with them both.

Many of us upon release would continue this relationship as functional members of the masjid: learning, teaching and providing whatever time, energy and resources we could. In those days, there was a core group of Brothers and Sisters who provided the creative energy and drive within the masjid. My primary function was to help with safety and security and also assist with the food cooperative project. Separately, there was a foundation set up which operated a day-care and child development program for Muslim and non-Muslim alike. At some point, I was appointed as the senior security officer for the masjid which increased my duties and responsibilities.

Around this time, our masjid or mosque agreed to be part of a coalition of Muslim groups and/or masajid called the Islamic Federation of North America (IFNA). This required cooperative agreements and relationships between the various groups and I was really impressed with the development I witnessed throughout our travels. In particular were the communities of Cleveland and New York (I think Brooklyn). The Muslim community in Cleveland for example had a housing development, businesses and an independent school or 'madrassah'. The New York masjid had a few businesses which created jobs for members of the community. I believe that they too, had a school. It was indeed an impressive display of the power of Islamic unity, purposeful leadership and strategic planning. Not to mention the fact that the leadership and Muslim communities were Black/New Afrikan and composed of working-class and low-income Black folks. Some, like myself, had even been formerly incarcerated.

During this period, I think many predominately Black/New Afrikan orthodox (Sunni, Shia) groups were really struggling around issues of identity and political direction. The Muslims under the leadership of Warith Deen Muhammad were still struggling to redefine themselves and establish their identity within the Islamic world, although they represented the singular largest group of Black/New Afrikan Muslims in the U.S. There was a confluence of forces from the Islamic world who were attempting to control the narrative and spread of Islam within the Black community.

The Nation of Islam (NOI) no longer represented the singular most dominant and visible expression of what it meant to be Black and Muslim in America and various forces from Saudi Arabia, Egypt, Pakistan and Iran were aggressively targeting and organizing within the New Afrikan/Black demographic.

The Saudis' had the advantage of not just enormous oil wealth, but favorable business and diplomatic relationships with the U.S. ruling class. Psychologically or subjectively, their strongest advantage was being the historical birthplace of Islam as taught by the Prophet Muhammad (PBUH), site of the first Islamic city-state (Medina) and custodian of the Holy City of Mecca and Islam's holiest shrine, the Kabah.

Egypt was highly regarded because of the ideological and organizational influence of the Muslim Brotherhood. Many of us had read Hasan Al-Bannah while we were incarcerated and were impressed with their dedication and ability to provide what appeared to be a more balanced and nuanced perspective between religious, political and social life.

Others had originally been exposed to orthodox Islam through the teachings of the Ahamdiyyah Movement via Ghulam Ahmad of Qadian, India: a 19th century Muslim who claimed to be the Mahdi or a divine reformer. As a matter of fact, older Black Muslims had originally transitioned from the NOI to the Ahamdiyyah Movement.

Much more influential were the 20th century teachings and writings of Abul A'la Maududi of the Jamaati Islami (Islamic Party) of Pakistan because of their focus on Islam as a political base and foundation for liberation and social transformation.

Some of us were paying close attention to the Islamic Republic of Iran because of their heroic and successful struggle to oust the forces of European colonialism and neo-colonialism (the Shah) and regain control of their country. Iran was also a nation that offered both political and material support to Blacks within the United States, most notably during and after certain urban rebellions (1980, 1989) in Florida.

And, last but certainly not least, were the pronouncements and sayings found in Libyan leader Muamar Gadhafi's 'Green Book', a sort of Islamic counter point to Chairman Mao's famous 'Red Book'. Under Gadhafi's leadership, Libya provided international recognition to the oppression experienced by Blacks/New Afrikans and also offered political and material support.

It appeared that many Black orthodox Muslims, in their zeal to embrace and practice traditional Islam and also distinguish themselves from the reactionary type Black Nationalism of the NOI, had themselves embraced a reactionary and apolitical form of Islamic ideology and practice. This was the type of thinking and practice which denounced any demonstration of racial consciousness and/or political activism which called into question prevailing systems and structures of white-supremacy. Any Black/New Afrikan Muslim who did so was denounced and labeled as 'nationalist', 'a kufr'(unbeliever) and would find themselves marginalized within the Muslim 'Ummah' or community.

The early 1980's witnessed the arrival and development of cult-of-personality masajid (mosques) based on allegiance to one particular sheikh or another and their interpretations and applications of Islam. For example, the Sheikh Gilani phenomenon called Muslims of America.

The faith, dedication and tenacity of New Afrikan/Black Muslims were being exploited to serve everyone's interest but our own. We actually had Brothers who wouldn't support a demonstration against police brutality at home because it represented 'nationalism', but would volunteer to go overseas and train to fight against the USSR in Afghanistan.

Against this backdrop, the idea of organizing a confederation of mostly Black/New Afrikan Muslims was welcome and much appreciated. However, the politics, objectives and leadership of those involved appeared to have changed and the initiative fizzled out. It would take several years for that awareness and spirit to be resurrected again during the 2000's in the call and formation of groups like the Muslim Alliance of North America (MANA). Meanwhile, the influence and power of the Salafi Movement was already upon our doorstep. May Allah give us all guidance and mercy. Ameen.

CHAPTER 4

Jesse Jackson's Presidential Campaigns: 1984 & 1988

I didn't contribute anything of too much significance to either campaign except that I both supported and voted for Jesse Jackson in both primaries. The National Black Independent Political Party (NBIPP) officially had no dog in either race, being ineffective in 1984 or non-existent by 1988.

The platform of the 1988 Jackson campaign was by far the most radical and progressive among all Democratic Party candidates seeking the nomination. At that moment in United States history, Jesse Jackson was hands-down the very best and most qualified candidate to represent the Democratic Party. However, the racism and fear of the Democratic Party leadership and segments of its constituency prevented them from grasping this fact.

Instead, they nominated Michael Dukakis and were soundly defeated by George H.W. Bush.

Jackson was popular enough to have posed a very serious and formidable challenge to the Democratic Party if he would have decided to break away and establish the 'Rainbow Coalition' as a third party. This would have provided yet another opportunity and platform for Blacks to challenge and free ourselves from the political trap-house of mainstream politics.

PART 2

1991-2000

- **African American United Front**
- **Campaign for a New Tomorrow**
- **Community Mosque, Inc.**
- **Gang Peace Council of Western PA**
- **National Council for Urban Peace and Justice**
- **Million Man March local Mobilization Committee & the MMM**
- **Justice for Jonny E. Gammage**
- **October 22nd Coalition**
- **Jericho '98**

CHAPTER 5

African-American United Front (AAUF):

Sometime in the early 1990's a group of Black activists from the Pittsburgh area began to meet and discuss the possibilities of forming a broad-based coalition to address our issues. All of us were deeply influenced by the recent re-emergence of interest in the life and politics of Malcolm X, the suppressed and inspiring radical legacy of Dr. King and what appeared to be the dismantling of apartheid in South Africa. We recognized that it was important to reach across the barriers of ideology, religion, culture and neighborhood to develop a unique organization that could speak to the multitude of challenges we faced collectively. Under the leadership of Rick Adams and others, the African-American United Front was created.

A few of us were also veterans from previous formations such as the NBIPP, while others were relatively new faces such as Rashid Sundiata, Randall Taylor, Sister Karen and Larry Hasan to name a few. We adopted the iconic photo of the first and only meeting between Martin Luther King, Jr. and Malcolm X as our official logo because it symbolized the importance of unity between and among the various elements within the Black or New Afrikan community. We conducted a series of community meetings and committee sessions which resulted in an impressive platform and structural document. Rashid Sundiata played a crucial role in this process. Along with Rick Adams, I was elected to serve as a co-Chairman of the AAUF to help with the facilitation of our work. One of our major challenges as a relatively new organization involved the police shooting of Duwayne Dixon in 1992.

On February 21, 1992 in what was described by police and the district attorney's office as a drug sweep, some sort of confrontation ensued involving Wilkinsburg police and 26 year old Wilkinsburg resident Duwayne Dixon and 27 year old Leroy McClendon, also of Wilkinsburg. In the end, Dixon was shot several times in what his mother and others described as a police initiated execution. Besides ad hoc protest and demonstrations involving a racist business owners interaction with a Black woman in East Liberty, the police killing of Duwayne Dixon would be the most serious, contentious and complex encounter for the embryonic AAUF. Robert Colville was then the district attorney for Allegheny County.

The killing of Dixon became a highly controversial case that cast a spotlight on the role of undercover police work, entrapment, the power of the coroners' report and the relationship between the police department and the district attorneys' office. It also featured Bob Pitts, the mayor of

Wilkinsburg who was a well-known and highly respected former civil rights activist that some among the AAUF knew personally. While Mayor Pitts publicly emphasized the importance of public confidence in public safety, he knew all too well the tendency of police to act improperly and violently when interacting with Black people, especially young Black males.

The basic police story was that they (police) approached Dixon and McClendon about drugs, a confrontation ensued with Dixon who was shot several times by the undercover police and once by his own gun which somehow became dislodged and discharged accidentally. The other interesting thing about the tragic death of Duwayne Dixon is that it literally featured a former civil rights activist, now the mayor of an economically declining and increasingly Black municipality, with a history of Jim Crow and KKK activity, adamantly supporting and defending the actions of an undercover drug task force that routinely profiled and targeted Black youth. On the other hand and in stark contrast, we find Bob Colville, a white district attorney for Allegheny County, publicly criticizing not only this state-initiated drug task force, but questioning the process, procedures, operations and training of its personnel.

The African American United Front held a series of meetings and discussions regarding the murder of Duwayne Dixon to work on information gathering and strategy. We decided to hold public protest and demonstrations, most notably, in front of the Wilkinsburg Municipal Building. Many people were angry and upset about the killing of Duwayne Dixon and there were rumors of possible violent protests. The AAUF made it clear that we encouraged all protestors and demonstrators to remain peaceful and focus on delivering our demands for an independent investigation and justice for the Dixon family.

To my surprise and the surprise of others, about two-days before the scheduled demonstrations, I got a telephone call from Mayor Bob Pitts. He too had concerns about the scheduled demonstrations and wanted some type of personal assurances that they would not be violent. I'm sure that Rick Adams probably got the same telephone call, since I believe that they had a much more personal and longer relationship. Nevertheless, I assured him that our intent was to engage in a series of non-violent protest and demonstrations in demanding justice for the family of Duwayne Dixon. Our goal was not to tear up or burn down the Wilkinsburg Municipal Building, nor encourage people to throw bricks and bottles at the police.

After all was said and done, the jury selected as part of the coroner's inquest was deadlocked as to whether the killing of Duwayne Dixon was accidental, justifiable homicide or murder. There would be no justice for the family and friends of Duwayne Dixon. Bob Pitts would continue to serve as mayor of Wilkinsburg for several more years and afterwards support civil rights and humanitarian work throughout Allegheny County until his death.

The killing of Duwayne Dixon and the ensuing controversy and politics demonstrates the failures and shortcomings of the civil rights movement: protest politics versus neo-colonial governance and the need for deeper and fundamental challenges to the status-quo.

The African-American United Front would continue to function for the next several months, but eventually fade away and dissolve. Many of its members would become involved in other groups and social justice campaigns over the years: some would go on to work in social services, education and non-profit management.

District Attorney Bob Colville had weathered the storm of a highly controversial police-involved shooting and demonstrated a tendency to be receptive to criticism and reforms in the process. However, the most controversial and polarizing case of his prosecutorial career was just a few years away: the 1995 police murder of Jonny Gammage.

CHAPTER 6

Campaign for a New Tomorrow:

Although the National Black Independent Political Party (NBIPP) was no longer functioning, the idea and passion for independent Black political activism remained. Under the leadership and direction of Ron Daniels, Campaign for a New Tomorrow was developed as an organizing vehicle and engine for a larger, more comprehensive movement for Black liberation and social justice. Its platform and program were radical and progressive and reflected a political perspective I could easily embrace. In some ways, it represented what an electoral version of Jesse Jacksons' Rainbow Coalition could have been. My central contribution to the platform was concerning advocacy and support for political prisoners.

I believe this is about the time that I first met Claire Cohen, a Black radical activist and Quaker, originally from the Philadelphia area. Claire brought a lot of energy and intellectual perspective to the initiative as well as principled compassion. Running on the platform of Campaign for a New Tomorrow, Ron Daniels ran an independent campaign for the Presidency of the United States in 1992. It was indeed an audacious and bold initiative and demonstrated the tangible potential of developing an independent and radical alternative to both mainstream political parties, especially the Democrats.

Unfortunately, this would symbolize perhaps the last and final effort from among those associated with, representing or organizing the National Black Political Convention of 1972 to fulfill the historic demand for an independent Black political party.

CHAPTER 7

Community Mosque, Inc. (CMI)

I have always maintained a very receptive and positive relationship with the vast majority of the Islamic community in spite of my personal shortcomings or any ideological differences. However, I had become increasingly frustrated and disappointed with the lack of activism emanating from the Muslim community, specifically those of us who follow the 'Sunnah' or tradition of Prophet Muhammad (Peace Be Upon Him/PBUH).

Endless debates concerning the role of Islam in pursuit of social justice and freedom often denigrated or marginalized the oppression of Blacks/New Afrikans, while highlighting the conditions of Muslims in some other part of the world. Their struggles were legitimate, while the struggles of Blacks were defined as just 'nationalism' or based on 'kufr' (disbelief). Some Brothers and Sisters knew more about the politics of Afghanistan and Saudi Arabia than what was happening in their own city. Malcolm X's letter during his Hajj was weaponized and used to suppress any discussion regarding racism among Muslims and the urgency of combating not just **white-supremacy**, but **Arab-supremacy** as well.

During this period, I began to seriously consider starting a study group or mosque that would center the teachings and practices of Islam on the historical and contemporary conditions of Black or New Afrikan people within the United States. I was well aware of groups such as the Mosque of Islamic Brotherhood, the Ansaruallah Muslim Community (led by Imam Issa) and Community Mosque-Atlanta, led by Imam Jamil Abdullah Al-Amin (H. Rap Brown). In previous years, myself and other incarcerated Muslims had made contact with and established relationships with most of these and other groups (in existence at that time), such as the Islamic Party of North America, in our search and journey to reconcile our political consciousness with our understanding and practice of Islam. Sometime in 1991, I began to share my perspective with other Muslims within the area, oftentimes during or after an Islamic studies session or discussion group.

In late 1991, I launched Community Mosque, Inc. as an Islamic study group that would serve as the prototype for an activist, radical and revolutionary Muslim configuration (or mosque) committed to centering Islam as the most suitable vehicle for personal and social transformation within the Black community. The first official member and facilitator was a brother from the Northside of Pittsburgh named Umar or 'Red' (aka Richard Williams). We met at the masjid in East Liberty and quickly became friends. In those days, Umar was a prolific street merchant, traveling to New York regularly to purchase wholesale cultural products that he then sold retail on the streets and sidewalks of Pittsburgh and surrounding areas.

These were the days of progressive, afro-centric and militant Hip-hop along with an assortment of Islamic literature, Free Nelson Mandela gear, Malcolm X shirts: videos, tapes, books and lectures on Afro-centrism along with Black history and culture. Brother Umar was also a gifted and talented musician and knew a lot of folks involved in the creative and performing arts. Our network and the reach of our messaging expanded greatly through his endorsement and participation as a member of Community Mosque, Inc.

As others expressed interest and joined our group we began to hold regular meetings at my apartment on the Northside. I served as the Imam for the group although it was certainly a position I neither coveted nor felt qualified to hold. I saw myself as more of an organizer, catalyst or convener. Fortunately for us, Brother Tariq Ismaeli joined CMI and agreed to serve as our first Amir. He was firmly grounded in Islamic traditions, spoke and read Arabic and had immense experience as both an instructor and administrator of Islamic programs and projects. He also was someone who was familiar with the local history of Black community organizing particularly within the eastern side of Pittsburgh, notably Homewood. Sister Amina Bey from the East Hills area and Sister Najwah who lived on the Northside were also key players in getting us off the ground and involved in the communities overall. A young brother by the name of Naeem Abu-Bakr joined as well. We adopted a platform that was based on many of the same social issues outlined by the Black Panther Party but within the context of Islamic principles and practice.

We also made it clear that we were not going to involve ourselves in the relatively petty sectarianism and ideological hair-splitting which was becoming so prevalent among our Muslim sisters and brothers. As Black people, we realized the importance of building principled working relationships with others within our tribe in order to more effectively and efficiently combat white supremacy and racist oppression. Our initial literature always made a point to recognize the existence and contributions of other Muslim movements, groups and organizations in developing Islamic identity among Black/New Afrikan peoples…even if we did not necessarily agree with their understanding or practice.

Eventually we started a little newsletter and magazine called the 'Movement'. It highlighted various events and activities within the area and featured news, editorials and our platform. Along with selling various cultural items donated by Brother Umar we had a fundraising dinner in the Homewood neighborhood as a way to spread the word and raise money. Around this time, there were several noticeable changes going on with Black youth in our area. We started noticing that slowly, but surely many kids started wearing the same colored clothing and hanging together in larger than usual crowds. We also started to notice the various messaging and graffiti that was sprawled on numerous walls and abandoned buildings. I had seen and experienced this all before growing up in Philadelphia back in the day. Other members of CMI had similar experiences and observations as well. It was straight up gang stuff: the colors and graffiti. Kids were mobbing up out of fear, excitement and protection.

The CMI Campaign for 'gang peace'

Within Community Mosque, we began to have serious discussions about how to respond to this growing crisis among and between our youth. We decided that it was important for us to educate the community and share with parents, teachers and community stakeholders' information regarding gang culture and intervention strategies. We also called for an area wide 'gang peace' campaign which involved direct community and personal outreach to the youth themselves. These were ideas I had formulated based on my experiences growing up in Philadelphia and through years of incarceration. I had borne witness to the work of groups such as the House of Umoja, Nation of Islam and Black Panther Party as well as the transformative power of Islam in general. Thus, I began to conduct and facilitate a series of informational workshops in various neighborhoods throughout the Pittsburgh area.

One evening after finishing up a presentation at the Homewood library, a brother approached me and indicated that he wanted to know how he could get involved. He expressed that he too, was greatly concerned about the escalating violence and gang affiliation impacting Black youth. We talked for just a few moments and discovered that we had much in common: we both had been members of the Black Panthers, were Muslims and had been formerly incarcerated. This is how I met Brother Rashad Byrdsong. I think this was around the fall of 1992. We hit it off right away and became friends and comrades. He joined CMI and added an extra valued dimension to our work through his organizing experience and military background as a Vietnam era veteran. He agreed to serve as our Amir of Security.

This is also around the time that I was working at a community based social service agency in the Hill district. Richard Garland, a friend and native Philadelphian who also had recently been released from prison worked there as well. A major component of our work involved working with so-called 'at-risk youth' throughout the school district and associated neighborhoods. This provided us with an opportunity to provide counseling and mentoring services and conduct prevention and intervention strategies for students involved in various conflicts.

In 1992, while attending a community event at the old Southern Platter restaurant, I had the opportunity to hear about an upcoming national summit regarding gang violence to be held in Kansas City sometime in 1993. The person who was delivering the information to the audience was a veteran peace and human rights activist named Molly Rush from the Thomas Merton Center. When I spoke with her later, I discovered that the convener of this summit was no other than Carl Upchurch. Carl Upchurch was an old friend and associate from prison. He had been incarcerated at Western state penitentiary and was also part of our student-prisoner crew that took classes thru the local college and university. He too, was originally from Philadelphia, but was paroled to somewhere in Ohio.

Carl and I stayed in touch when he first came home from prison, but eventually lost touch after a few years. I was excited to reconnect with him and hear his ideas about the projected outcome for the upcoming summit. I shared with him information concerning the escalating and deadly proliferation of gang-related violence throughout the Pittsburgh area and my ideas about how to proceed. We agreed that Pittsburgh should be represented at the scheduled Gang Peace Summit in 1993 and Carl encouraged me and others to attend.

Within the mosque, we reached consensus that a contingent of CMI members would attend the first National (Gang Peace) Urban Peace and Justice Summit in Kansas City, Missouri in late April of 1993. As Community Mosque, Inc., we also agreed to continue the work of implementing the local 'gang peace' program. As we neared the date for the summit in Kansas, we ran into financial difficulties in being able to transport and house the original number of people who had agreed to attend. I was able to secure financial support from my employer (Addison Terrace Learning Center). Stephanie Ezekoye served as executive director, with Sylvia Nanji, Cathy McGee, Victoria Grant and others providing strong administrative and staff support throughout the agency. I was also able to secure financial support from the progressive Three Rivers Community Foundation. In the final analysis, due to financial and personal hardship, only two of us would be able to attend the summit, Rashad and myself.

So, sometime in late April of 1993, we boarded a plane for Kansas City in search of hope, inspiration and ideas in the battle against the destructive forces of racism, capitalism, sexism and the self/group hatred epitomized through gang and drug related violence.

Kansas City Summit:

There was already a flurry of activity by the time we arrived. People from various parts of the country were streaming in representing all types of groups, organizations and movements including civil rights organizations, youth development groups, clergy of every denomination imaginable: gang-sets, individual gang members, local, national and international media, public officials, etc. And in spite of their negative commentaries and cynicism concerning the possibilities for positive outcomes resulting from this historic gathering, I'm sure that there were police and law enforcement forces there too.

Carl Upchurch was extremely busy: managing multiple tasks while attempting to be welcoming and hospitable to all those representatives, delegates and participants checking it, particularly those whom he had been working with over the last several months or knew personally. Before I could even speak with Carl and let him know that we had arrived, I had to go touch base with this brother from LA, sporting his blue and looking real serious and not very welcoming. His name was Big Al and close by was his friend and homeboy Elementary. These were the first people we met upon arriving at the registration and check in site for the summit.

After greeting and having a quick chit-chat with Carl, Rashad and I went outside just to check out the atmosphere. Because we both had on kufis, I suspect that may have prompted the two brothers coming up the street to approach us and ask about check in and registration. Although obviously a little tired and traveled, they were both striking and dignified in their posture and Afro-Islamic garb. One brother, average in height, began seeking directions. The other, who appeared to be much taller, provided the reinforcements. This is how we first met Omar Ali Bey and Khalid Samad, from Cleveland. Because we were all Muslims as well as activists, we connected easily.

Carl Upchurch had been traveling around the country for months meeting with various individuals, street organizations/gangs, activists, clergy and civil rights leaders in an effort to stop the escalating and national epidemic of urban violence. He began this process from the small town of Granville, Ohio: rallying support for the initiative and forming a local group called the **Council for Urban Peace and Justice**. He had been greatly influenced and inspired by the truce between some Crips and Bloods shortly before the 1992 urban insurrection in Los Angeles. He envisioned a national duplication of this model with the initial gathering to occur at the 1993 summit in Kansas City, Missouri. It was a long-shot, but Carl decided that the lives of current and future generations were certainly worth the risk, sacrifice and hard work.

There were numerous gang sets and street organizations represented at the 1st National Gang Peace Summit: Bloods, Crips, Vice-Lords, Latin Kings, Disciples, Stones, Mexican Mafia, Texas Syndicate, etc. of all races and ethnicities: Black, White, Brown, Indigenous, Asian. Some had women representatives play key and crucial roles, but patriarchy and male chauvinism was a profound and dominant tendency during the summit which continued to need redress. However, among certain Latino/Hispanic formations such as Barrios Unidos, there was noticeably much more balance, inclusiveness and democracy regarding the role of women and girls.

The summit agenda was radical, progressive and audacious. It was to be organized and led by a coalition of former gang-members, current gang- members, formerly incarcerated people: activists of all colors and stripes, radical clergy of every denomination and spiritual tendency imaginable: a select group of public officials, academics and small business owners. Key areas to be addressed via workshops and team building were: negotiating an end to the violence within our communities and developing new models for resolving conflict: developing political power for our people: jobs and economic development for our communities: ending the relentless injustices experienced by our communities in areas such as housing, health care, police brutality and criminal justice.

The women attending the summit caucused in order to specifically address issues of sexism, male chauvinism, patriarchy and misogyny. Of particular concern were the negative portrayals of girls and women in the music and entertainment industry as well as the male chauvinism exhibited by male participants, including some leadership during the summit. They formed their own and separate component called 'Sisters of the Summit', which provided a vehicle for them to advocate, lobby and propose specific policies regarding women and girls within our communities. I had a chance to meet and dialogue with women such as journalist, writer and activist Margie Hollins from St. Louis, Sister Zephirah Muhammad from Cleveland, Sister 'Chi' from Minneapolis, the women of Barrios Unidos, Najma Nazgat of Boston, etc.

The summit was able to attract and secure the attention and support of Ben Chavis, himself a former political prisoner, who had been selected as the new executive director of the national NAACP. Even though more conservative elements within some civil rights circles (including then former and current NAACP leadership) felt uncomfortable with Bens' politics, he was most definitely a breath of fresh air that brought a more dynamic, militant, youthful and relevant face to the organization. Most importantly, his endorsement gave the summit additional legitimacy within certain activist circles. It also helped to raise needed resources as well. Likewise, the support and endorsement of Minister Farrakhan and the Nation of Islam was also very significant, particularly among the more militant, Black Nationalist elements within the community. Politically, the summit had the support and endorsement of Mayor Emmanuel Cleaver (who later became a U.S. Congressman), which also gave it added legitimacy and opened up some doors that otherwise would have been closed.

Such an undertaking was bound to have various challenges: programmatic, logistical, financial and social. One such problem was actually created by local media covering the summit who managed to manipulate a group of young gang-members into giving an interview that was hostile to the message and organizers of the summit. Our immediate response was to go out into the community and engage the youth and others. Next, we called out the media responsible for the attempted sabotage and banned them from the next press conference. And, finally we convened a special, closed door meeting directly with the young homies involved to review the dangers of media manipulation, sabotage and COINTELPRO type activities.

I met several people who would emerge as key leaders within the then embryonic urban peace and justice movement: former Black Panther Sister Marion Stamps from Chicago, Wallace 'Gator' Bradley, Spike Moss, Sharif Willis, Martin Talamante, Prince Asiel of the Black Hebrew Nation, Nane' Alejandrez, Jitu Sadiki, Fanya Baruti, Rodney Dailey, Rahim Jenkins and many more too numerous to list and several more whose names I can't recall.

I also would be remiss without mentioning the overwhelming support the summit received from the religious community in the area, especially, the Rev. Mack Charles Jones of St. Stephens Church and Rev. Sam Mann of St. Mark Union Church. Church members provided food, comfort and housing to several summit attendees. The majority of the summit activities were held at St. Stephens Church. Brother Rashad and I stayed with a Christian family the entire time we were in Kansas City. They were very hospitable and warm people with a great sense of humor as well. They even had a Pittsburgh connection in that they were related to a family that ran a barbeque joint on the Northside.

In the closing hours of the summit, attendees and representatives resolved to come together as a national body or coalition under the name **National Council for Urban Peace and Justice**. We agreed to meet in various cities and locations around the country in the upcoming months ahead. We would continue the process of organizing and facilitating peace, reconciliation, justice and human development.

CHAPTER 8

The Gang Peace Council of Western Pennsylvania: (GPC)

On the return flight to Pittsburgh, Rashad and I reflected and processed the events of the past few days. We knew there was much work to be done in Pittsburgh and were inspired by the sheer volume of national energy and unity we would now be part of. I knew I had to be responsible for a least four reports: one to the members of CMI: my employer (and co-workers) who provided financial, logistical and moral support: the Three Rivers Community Foundation for providing financial and political support: and last, but most importantly…the communities that we represented at the summit.

It was agreed that we needed to expand the gang-peace work being done by Community Mosque Inc. to include a much broader group of people, a local coalition. We needed to call ourselves something since those joining would not all necessarily be members of CMI.

I liked the term 'gang peace' because it was associated with the campaign we had previously started, but I found out during the summit that there was already a group based in Boston and started by Rodney Dailey called 'Gang Peace'. They were a great organization and had developed a solid reputation for organizing street youth and creating innovative programs, including job training and entrepreneurial projects. So after some discussion, it was decided to call our coalition the 'Gang Peace Council of Western Pennsylvania'. Eventually, most people throughout the area would come to identify us as simply the Gang Peace Council.

Now we had to set about the task of recruiting and organizing people into this new initiative. As Muslims, the first group of people we attempted to recruit were other sisters and brothers from among the Islamic community. We were very successful. Individual members from the Nation of Islam joined: so did the followers of Imam Warith Deen Muhammad, the Ahamdiyyah Movement, members of both the First Muslim Mosque (Masjid al Awwal) and Masjid al Mu'min joined as well: and the entire Moorish Science Temple via its Secretary signed up! In the early weeks of recruitment the Gang Peace Council was exclusively a Muslim organization.

We could no longer meet over my Northside apartment so we started to gather at different locations based on availability. One of our regular meeting places was the YMCA in Homewood under the secure and watchful eye of Brother Elijah, who worked there. It was at one of these meetings that the first non-Muslim requested to join the

GPC. He was a brother that many of us knew as a Black Nationalist and Pan-Africanist who also lifted weights and worked out with Brother Elijah. He happened to be in the lobby the day of our meeting and asked could he stay, participate and join. We nodded our heads in consensus and that was the beginning of our general membership recruitment.

Another popular meeting site was the University of Pittsburgh. At Pitt, we were able to recruit and involve students, particularly those associated with the Black Action Society. This is where I first met Brother Kwame Scott who would emerge as one of the most important and significant persons of the gang peace movement for many years to come. The first white person to join the GPC was a doctor of psychiatry named Bob Marin, probably followed shortly thereafter by another doctor, Bob Connamacher who was a member and advocate from the Pennsylvania Prison Society. Bob Connamacher was also heavily involved with recruiting Black students and other students of color into Pitts' medical school.

Meanwhile, the work I was doing through my job at Addison Terrace Learning Center gave me an opportunity to interact with hundreds of mostly middle and high school students who were either involved or living in neighborhoods experiencing the constant gang shootings and other violence. The connection between the communities and the schools was profound. Conflicts could begin in one and easily spread to the other. These were the years of pagers or beepers and modern communications technology would prove to be a crucial tool in violence prevention and intervention. The youth on the streets had learned how to use it effectively too. Along with the dickies, bandanas and flannel shirts, it became a part of the hustle and the imagery. Having such a dynamic and innovative staff which included me, Richard Garland, Shirley Muhammad, Sidney Williams, Roger Green, Denise Giles, Debbie Young, Leonard Pinkney and Brother Kevin, our agency (Addison Terrace Learning Center) was in high demand regarding gang violence prevention and intervention.

In between work hours, the Gang Peace Council remained busier than ever: going into the various neighborhoods, meeting with the youth, negotiating 'cease fires', truces (often temporary): attending and speaking at funerals, trying to comfort distraught parents, family and friends/homies…some of whom wanted immediate retaliation and revenge. Doing regular home visits with traumatized students and young adults: trying to deal with parents and adults who were truly dysfunctional and unable to take care of themselves, let alone parent a child. Young drug dealers/homeboys fighting for survival and against rival neighborhoods. Many would fall victim to either bullets or prison. Later, some would fall victim to the very drugs they once sold and hustled. Against this backdrop were politicians, law enforcement and public officials who engaged in what I refer to as the politics of denial. As far as some of them were concerned, there was no gang problem in Pittsburgh and Allegheny County, just a bunch of copy cats and wannabe gang-bangers. They saw it as just a phase of juvenile transgression that would quickly pass. Meanwhile, children and young adults were being murdered and maimed in record numbers. For example, 1993 set an unprecedented record for murders and shootings in Pittsburgh and Allegheny County. Fortunately, there were some voices on Pittsburgh city council who understood the seriousness and enormity of the situation our communities were dealing with.

On the other hand, the Pittsburgh Board of Education was actually proactive and receptive to innovative and creative strategies to curb and reduce gang violence. Unlike city and county politicians, the school districts had been dealing directly with the young people involved and impacted on a daily basis. I facilitated workshops and discussions sponsored by parent advisory groups and student services. Later, the school district would convene and facilitate a task force composed of city, county, law enforcement, activists, parents, and social service providers specifically to address the violence.

The person I credit with a lot of these developments was Janet Yuhaz from Student Services. Janet would be our central contact and point person at the Pittsburgh school district for many years. She remained dedicated and committed to helping students and families get the most from the experience of public education and maintaining a safe environment. Another important staffer from Pittsburgh Student Services was Harriet Meriwether who worked closely with Janet. We are indebted to her as well. Next up would be participation and attendance in the urban peace and justice summits in Cleveland and Chicago during the remainder of 1993.

Cleveland Summit:

The Cleveland summit was hosted and organized by Coalition for a Better Life & Peace In the Hood, organizations represented by Omar Ali Bey and Khalid Samad. Held in early June of 1993, the summit was very well attended and featured speakers ranging from Cleveland mayor Michael White, Congressman Stokes to Imam Jamil Abdullah Al-Amin. Many of the key representatives from the Kansas City summit were there as well, lending logistical support and solidarity.

By this time, the Gang Peace Council of Western PA was the official name of the Pittsburgh-based group. If I recall correctly, Rashad was unable to make this trip or arrived later, so I traveled with another Muslim brother by the name of Walter Shahid from Masjid An-Nur. It was during this particular summit that I recall the first time I heard Carl Upchurch mention a proposal to organize a march on Washington to address the economic links to the violence we were experiencing within our communities nationwide.

He talked about the gross income disparities between Blacks and whites, particularly the high unemployment rates among Black youth. He suggested a Million Youth March for Jobs and Economic Justice. This was during a closed meeting and discussion with representatives and some guest speakers in attendance, including Dick Gregory, Nation of Islam (NOI) Chief of Staff Leonard Muhammad and, perhaps Imam Jamil (I don't recall if the Imam attended this meeting or just waited outside until the march and rally later). It is my belief that this is actually where the concept and idea for the Million Man March originated.

Chicago Summit:

Although we were not able to attend the summit in Minneapolis, we were excited and energized based on the information and reports we heard from others. However, by the late summer of 1993, we had recruited enough members and galvanized sufficient support to sponsor a group of local gang representatives as participants in the Chicago summit.

We hoped that this contingent of young people, removed from the immediate threats and dangers of the Pittsburgh streets, would find some positive and inspiring examples among Chicago youth they could connect and relate to. After all, since the tragic killing of seven year old Dantrell Davis in 1992, gang forces in the Cabrini Green housing complex and elsewhere had agreed to a cease fire. This involved gangs such as the Vice Lords and Gangster Disciples who had a history of inflicting serious murder and mayhem among themselves. Led by community members, especially Black women, such as activist and former Black Panther Marion Stamps, the people demanded an end to gang and drug related violence. The type of violence which had been spiraling out of control and now had taken the life of a seven-year old child.

The Chicago summit was sponsored and facilitated by a host of people and organizations including United In Peace (Wallace 'Gator' Bradley), No Dope Express Foundation (Earl King) and the Black Hebrew Israelites, represented by Prince Asiel Ben Israel. Ben Chavis and Minister Farrakhan supported the summit and were expected to attend and speak. Jesse Jackson and Operation PUSH also pledged their support. In addition, various politicians and public officials had been invited, in spite of their unsolicited criticism, cynicism and negative commentary.

Lester Cain, a veteran educator and activist from the Pittsburgh area, and his wife, community activist Lois Cain supported our plans to attend the Chicago summit. They were able to convince Congressman Bill Coyne to provide financial assistance and moral support as well.

As we began organizing to attend the Chicago summit, we knew that security was of utmost importance. We were able to secure two or three passenger vans in order to provide transportation for the over dozen youth and support staff needed. The facilitator and mentor staff included Rashad Byrdsong, Richard Garland, Dewayne Muhammad (Sister Shirley Muhammad's son), a couple of other brothers and myself. We had youth representatives from the Northside, East Hills, Homewood and the Southside: Crips and Bloods.

I tried unsuccessfully to get some of the young people ('O.G.'s) from Manchester to attend. But because of a relatively recent incident, I understood why. However, they would later play an extremely key and important role in setting an example and standard for the entire movement in the Pittsburgh region.

Before officially hitting the road, we conducted a thorough weapons check and search (conducted by the Fruit of Islam/FOI). This was done early in the morning at the University of Pittsburgh's David Lawrence Hall. So, we embarked on this journey hoping to inspire and motivate our youth to seek and organize for peace and justice among themselves. It was late October of 1993.

The atmosphere among the youth was respectful, but tense. Some people knew or heard of one another: others were just meeting for the first time. It was a long trip, but in between rest stops, bathroom breaks and eating food, the atmosphere became more relaxed and open. Steve Drake did a lot to help keep the contingent of Crips focused; however, we still had a few moments.

As we got closer to the summit hotel, we got word about a protest and demonstration against the Chicago summit and everything it stood for. This demonstration had been organized and led by the Guardian Angels, a community safety and patrol organization started in New York City, but with members in Chicago and elsewhere. Apparently, they got caught up in the anti-summit politics and rhetoric of the police and some politicians who opposed the peaceful and purposeful gathering of gang members and activists in their city, no matter how righteous the intent. Perhaps they saw educated and organized gang members and ex-gang members as a threat to their 'territory' as a public safety group which had been receiving funds and recognition for several years. Who better to make peace and reduce violence than those who had been directly involved in it as perpetrators and victims; those who had direct and personal influence on the ebb and flow of street life and culture.

In response to the demonstrations, the Pittsburgh youth became angry and actually talked about fighting any Guardian Angels who attempted to block them from entering the summit hotel lobby. We explained to them that perhaps that is exactly what the Guardian Angels, their supporters and the media wanted them to do, in order to discredit the purpose and intent of the summit. They understood.

When we discharged from the vans and headed toward the hotel lobby, the Pittsburgh delegation ignored the demonstrators and remained focused and disciplined. This was a huge accomplishment. From this moment forward, the delegation was more focused and unified (although not necessarily as disciplined as they should be). Oddly, we owe a part of this to the reactionary politics and antics of the Guardian Angels and their backers. They forced the Pittsburgh delegation to think and act in unity.

The summit featured several workshops centered on the general principles of the national coalition such as conflict resolution, social justice, economic justice, political empowerment and community development. However, our national group still needed to address issues of sexism, male chauvinism and patriarchy in a meaningful way. This would continue to remain a consistent problem and issue.

The Chicago summit also featured several memorable moments:

- a press conference involving the Pittsburgh delegation:

- a huge peace rally with representatives from various gangs/street organizations:
- the nationally (radio) broadcast meeting, fundraiser and voter registration drive held at the headquarters of Operation Push, again involving representatives of various street organizations:
- the gathering at Mosque Maryam with a powerful speech and presentation by Minister Farrakhan:
- And last, but not least, the peace party held at the Cabrini-Green housing complex with GD's and Vice Lords, in which the Pittsburgh delegates were the guest of honor.

On the way back to the steel city, the Pittsburgh delegation was very excited and enthusiastic concerning what they experienced in Chicago and the prospects for peace on the streets of Pittsburgh.

As the year came to an end, the Gang Peace Council continued its work, increased membership and expanded its network. 1993 became a benchmark year for gun violence throughout Pittsburgh and Allegheny County. It was time for an urban peace and justice (gang-peace) summit in Pittsburgh.

Pittsburgh Summit:

I began to float the idea of a Pittsburgh summit among the national leadership of the National Council for Urban Peace and Justice (NCUPJ) and our local members and supporters here within the Gang Peace Council. There was a mixture of support versus apprehension about taking on such an arduous task. It was eventually decided to move forward.

Unlike the summits in cities like Kansas City, Cleveland and San Antonio, the proposed gang-peace summit for Pittsburgh faced enormous political opposition. Law enforcement, Mayor Tom Murphy and a significant number of Pittsburgh City Council representatives were all vehemently opposed to it. Many continued to deny the existence of a serious gang problem in spite of the almost routine media reports of shootings and killings among and between various groups of youth.

It had gotten to the point where the shootings and drive-byes became predictable patterns of retaliatory violence. Shots would be fired in Homewood, shortly thereafter shots would be fired in East Hills or Larimer, or Garfield, on and on and on…,. These patterns had developed across the entire city of Pittsburgh and adjacent cities, boroughs and townships of Allegheny County as well. Wilkinsburg, McKeesport, Rankin, Braddock, Clairton, etc. were all going through the same thing.

Meanwhile, many public officials continued to play the fiddle while the neighborhoods burned, all the while casting shade and dispersion on the efforts, energies and strategies of those of us who were trying desperately to save our children and ourselves. Pittsburgh City Council actually voted on whether or not to endorse, welcome or support the summit.

The end result was a tie vote, only because a key supporter was ill. Our supporters were led by councilmen Rev. Duane Darkins and Jimmy Ferlo. Furthermore, the media attempted to castigate Councilman Darkins for providing us with a grant of twenty-five hundred dollars ($2,500.00) which they constantly misreported (lied about) as thousands of dollars more. It was a classic case of collusion between public officials and media in order to discredit a movement.

However, the support for a Pittsburgh gang-peace summit continued to gain momentum as various forces within the Black community embraced the idea. Women and mothers like Renee Goodson, Debbie Black and Cheryl Harvey who had lost children or family to street violence, led the charge in galvanizing youth and parents from affected communities. At this juncture, Renee was the Vice-President of the Gang-Peace Council. Years later, Debbie would serve as Vice-President of the NCUPJ.

Rev. Ron Peters from the Pittsburgh Theological Seminary and Rev. Jimmy Joe Robinson from the Bidwell Presbyterian Church played crucial and key roles in galvanizing moral and material support from the church community. The summit registration, workshops, opening and closing ceremonies were all hosted and convened by a consortium of churches in the Manchester neighborhood.

People poured in from all across the city and county: Northside, East End, Southside, Westside: South Oakland, the Hill, Hazelwood, Wilkinsburg, etc. They came on foot, in cars and vans: even large U-Haul trucks, most wearing their respective gang colors to represent. A lot of the outreach work and the hope and optimism for peace were due in part to the message and efforts of members of the Pittsburgh delegation that attended the Chicago summit. People from around the country began to flow in as well:

Cleveland, Chicago, Los Angeles, Philadelphia, Boston, Texas, Kansas City, etc.

My oldest brother, Harry (Bilal), an 'old head' from 'the Bottom' in West Philly was able to attend the summit. During a television interview with a local network, he talked about his experiences, our father and how hopeful he (Bilal) was that some good would come out of this gathering. The summit also attracted not just local media, but national and international alike, with correspondents, journalists and film crews from as far away as Finland.

The Pittsburgh summit was not without some disappointments and conflict, however. We had an incident involving someone, traveling outside one of the host churches, firing a shot into the air during a conflict resolution workshop. People, not sure as to what was going on, began to duck and scramble for a moment. Some ran to their vehicles for cover and escape. To the amazement of some, **all** the summit participants returned the following day to continue the process. We also had some verbal confrontations during one of the workshops, but experienced facilitators (mostly former and current gang -members from around the country) were able to resolve it.

But there were **no fights or bloodshed** during the Pittsburgh summit as had been predicted and publicized by certain politicians, law enforcement and media outlets. Nor, did gangs roam the streets of downtown Pittsburgh wreaking havoc and mayhem as forecast by political pundits and detractors. The Pittsburgh Urban Peace and Justice (Gang-Peace) Summit occurred from May 27th-29th of 1994. This was one of the most non-violent and peaceful weekends the

Pittsburgh area, especially the Black/New Afrikan community, had experienced in months.

Setting Up Shop:

After the Pittsburgh summit, the messaging and work of the GPC continued to expand with more and more demands on my personal time and energy. Sometime in late June or early July of 1994, I left my position at Addison Terrace Learning Center in order to devote my full time to developing and expanding the Gang Peace Council, in addition to my duties as the Secretary for the National Council for Urban Peace and Justice. Determined, but with very little personal funds or resources for organizational development, we solicited donations and volunteers.

We started looking for a small office space from which to officially operate and initially considered locations in Oakland (University of Pittsburgh area) and the Northside

(Three Rivers Stadium area). Our main concerns, in addition to costs were issues of safety, security and access. We wanted a location that was in a relatively 'neutral' location, unclaimed by any particular gang-set. No one was claiming the University of Pittsburgh area, although there was a set of Crips from the south Oakland neighborhood. The old Three Rivers Stadium area was also neutral territory. I contacted property managers to begin the process of securing a rental agreement, but as soon as I identified our group (Gang Peace Council of Western Pa.), I was told the space was no longer available or in some instances, telephone calls were just never returned.

We were finally able to secure a lease agreement with E.V. Bishoff Properties for a small office in downtown Pittsburgh. The rental fee was affordable and the location was centrally located in downtown Pittsburgh with public transportation available. It also placed our offices in walking distance from all government offices (City-County Building, Federal Building, Pennsylvania State Building) and some major media outlets (KDKA, Pittsburgh Post-Gazette). Most importantly, no one was 'claiming' or representing downtown Pittsburgh.

We moved into our new office in August of 1994. Our staff at this time were all volunteers and would eventually consist of Kwame Scott, Lloyd Adams, Celeste Banks, Naimah Abdullah, myself and a young mother from the McKeesport area named Theresa who served as the office manager and administrative assistant. Almost immediately we began to solicit donations in order to equip our office: telephones, fax machine, printers, desk top computers and an old, bulky (but quite effective) copier. Lois & Lester Cain even gave us an old mini fridge that one of their children had used in college!

Initially, Rashad Byrdsong was tasked with coordinating and organizing Gang Peace Council work in the East End (Homewood, Larimer, East Hills, Garfield, Wilkinsburg), but decided to start his own organization, so we parted ways in the fall of 1994. Later, another friend and associate from prison; a former hustler from Pittsburgh's' Hill district, Jeffrey Dunmore would serve as coordinator for outreach activities. He would be supported by former gang members, community activists and students (mostly from Pitt) and other guys from prison.

Jeff was the one who introduced Elbert (El) Gray from the Northside to the organization. Like Kwame and a few others, El Gray would turn out to be one of the most important and impactful persons in the movement. A major part of our philosophy and practice was to facilitate the peace process and actively recruit former or current gang members to work as staff. Initially, they would serve as outreach workers and eventually move up into administrative, managerial or technical positions based on their interests and skill set.

This scenario would develop over the years as we transitioned from basically an advocacy/social justice organization into an advocacy/social justice **and** social services non-profit. In the early years, former gang members Mark Green and Brother Abdullah, a Gangster Disciple (G.D.) transplant from the south were some of our first recruits. Both had attended the Pittsburgh summit. Years later, another dynamic graduate from our program, former gang member, Perron Shepard would develop into a dedicated community organizer and youth advocate. Carol Frazier, a trained therapist and gifted gardener, organized and managed our urban gardening project titled 'Project Success'.

Student volunteers were also a major part of this process; particularly the students connected to Pitts' Black Action Society and similar type groups. Many eventually became paid staff. People like Aliya Durham and Desiree Lee: and later, paid staff like Malcolm Minnekhekh Thomas, Sister IAsia Thomas and others who expanded our work in the schools and the community as we became more program and project oriented. All of them made tremendous sacrifices; oftentimes overworked and underpaid, but never under appreciated.

The Gang Peace Council was a membership-based organization and our numbers were growing regularly. Youth, parents, activists, professionals, clergy, business people and public officials were all joining our ranks. I believe some were attempting to hijack and control our movement, but the overwhelming majority were sincerely trying to bring peace, justice and stability to our communities.

As we grew in numbers and influence, we were able to gradually secure additional funding which helped us to transition into social services provision. We modeled our social services on the guiding **principles** that we all had

agreed upon in forming and structuring the National Council for Urban Peace and Justice:

1. **Visions for our Future**
2. **Political Empowerment**
3. **Economic Development**
4. **Social Justice**
5. **Respect Women**

CHAPTER 9

The National Council for Urban Peace and Justice: NCUPJ

In August of 1993, we had a meeting and summit in the District of Columbia (D.C.) to coincide with the Southern Christian Leadership Conference (SCLC) awards dinner and 30th anniversary commemoration of the 1963 March on Washington.

Carl Upchurch was being recognized and cited for his work around criminal justice reform and the urban peace and justice movement. Rev. Joseph Lowery of the SCLC had attended and participated at the Minneapolis summit held earlier that year.

Carl extended an invitation to all the NCUPJ representatives that could attend. He wanted to make it clear that he was accepting the award on our behalf, but most importantly on behalf of those people in various cities who were working hard to keep the peace or attempting to create it. At this point, Carl was still able to solicit assistance from his workplace and network in Granville, Ohio in managing the organizational challenges of holding the NCUPJ together. Travel logistics, including air fare and hotel reservations were taken care of. The D. C. host organization, The Righteous Men's Commission didn't have much to do in that regard.

The awards dinner and conference featured recognition and comments from Rosa Parks, Rev. Lowery, Coretta Scott King, Jesse Jackson, President Aristides of Haiti and many leaders from SCLC chapters throughout the country. It was during this meeting that we adopted a basic structure for the National Council for Urban Peace and Justice, identifying and verifying member organizations, electing officers and assigning various tasks.

There were several individuals, groups and organizations that officially and publicly identified as members of the National Council for Urban Peace and justice, such as:

- **Council for Urban Peace and Justice: Granville, Ohio**
- **United In Peace: Chicago**
- **No Dope Express Foundation: Chicago**
- **Barrios Unidos: Santa Cruz**
- **United For Peace: Minneapolis**

- **The City: Minneapolis**
- **Black Hebrew Israelites: Chicago**
- **Black Awareness Community Development Organization: Los Angeles**
- **Coalition for a Better Life/Peace in the Hood: Cleveland**
- **Righteous Men's Commission: Washington, D.C.**
- **Gang Peace, Incorporated: Boston**
- **Gang Peace Council of Western Pennsylvania: Pittsburgh**

Each group or individual was represented on the council and we proceeded to select officers as well. Carl Upchurch was selected to serve as President; Prince Asiel Ben Israel as Vice President, and I was selected to serve as Secretary-Treasurer. The original selection for treasurer was scheduled to leave the country soon, unsure of his exact return. It was also decided that Pittsburgh would be the site of our national office and headquarters. A brother from the Righteous Men's Commission and I were tasked with the responsibility of compiling and organizing the suggestions and notes regarding structure and administration into a comprehensive document to be reviewed and ratified at a later date.

The women and girls of the National Council continued to push back concerning issues of male chauvinism and sexism. Utilizing the network and independent association they had formed in Kansas City **('Sisters of the Summit')**, they held a rally on the mall and formed their own parallel leadership council called the **'Council of Queens'**. The day of the anniversary march (August 28, 1993) was extremely hot. I had taken one of my children (Aisha) with me on this journey, and although she was probably hot, tired and hungry, she just held my hand tightly and marched on. But at some point, before we went inside the rotunda of the Lincoln Memorial, we both found some shade and rest. Someone from the Council of Queens (I think it was Sister Zephirah Muhammad) took Aisha aside, along with some other youth, as we prepared our entourage to represent and deliver our message.

There was a moment of controversy concerning who would represent and speak on behalf of the NCUPJ that day. Some people suggested that Ben Chavis speak on our behalf, since as executive director of the NAACP, he had paved the way for us to receive support and recognition. Furthermore, he was a nationally recognized leader who could make an impassioned plea in support of the movement. I interjected that while we certainly respect and appreciate Ben's help and history, Carl was our national spokesman and representative who was more than qualified to represent us. We all agreed and stood behind and next to Carl Upchurch: former gang-member, former hustler and formerly incarcerated person as he delivered an impassioned plea on behalf of urban America to an estimated audience of 75,000 people in front of the Lincoln Memorial on August 28, 1993. It was a long way from having discussions and debates while sitting around the prison yard in Western Penitentiary.

Male chauvinism and sexism continued to plague the organizational development of the National Council. Sisters were excluded from high level officer positions and often treated in a paternalistic and condescending manner. The prevalent misogynistic and sexually-exploitative gang culture would remain an ongoing challenge within the ranks of the young men (and women) we attempted to recruit to the movement. Much of it, I contend, reinforced by economic injustices and the cultures of street-hustle capitalism and predatory violence. I suspect that these concerns, among others, may have accounted for some of the tensions between Carl and Nane'. Barrios Unidos was a much more developed and disciplined organization than the NCUPJ, which at that point, was really no more than a national ad-hoc committee. I believe there also were some differences regarding both the direction and membership composition of the NCUPJ. Nevertheless, together, we all moved on. The next gathering or summit would be in Texas.

San Antonio Summit:

Weeks prior to the summit in San Antonio, Carl had introduced me to Rev. Anne Helmke of Grace Lutheran Church, site for the proposed gathering. Rev. Helmke was one of the central conveners and organizers. She was engaging, very hospitable, enthusiastic…and a great organizer. Before the summit, an advance team of NCUPJ mediators and facilitators traveled to San Antonio in order to get a feel for the environment and lay down some groundwork. I think Fanya Baruti of Black Awareness Community Development Organization (BACDO), Barrios Unidos and Daud Sherrill were part of this team.

By this time, we had incorporated the practice of visiting area schools, youth detention centers, prisons, community centers and certain neighborhood areas (before and after the summit) in order to spread the word, network and recruit people into the movement. We also made a point to organize and craft our media appearances and press conferences. We had quickly incorporated the lessons of previous media experiences such as what occurred with the young homies from Kansas City.

The Pittsburgh entourage included Richard Garland, Rashad

Byrdsong, myself and Steven Cryor. Steve was another formerly incarcerated person who worked as a youth and substance abuse counselor in the Pittsburgh area. Originally from West Philly, he was a friend and former gang member from my old neighborhood in the 'Bottom'.

During the summit weekend, we had an opportunity to visit various communities, one of which included the East Terrace neighborhood. There, we met and networked with a crew called the 'East Terrace Gangsters' (ETG) who wanted to participate in the summit, but still had some challenges to address, particularly the willingness of other gangs to participate and respect a truce.

Overall, the San Antonio summit was successful in attracting hundreds of people; and garnering the support of, not just clergy and activists, but public officials and business people too. But most importantly, it resulted in several gangs in the area agreeing to a truce and a cessation of violence. The impact was an immediate decrease in shootings, aggravated assaults and murders.

(Top photo: Cleveland Summit)

(Bottom photo: San Antonio Summit)

Growing Pains:

Moving beyond organizing and convening gang peace summits, the greater work of the National Council had to involve both program and policy development. We needed to address key questions of strategic planning and direction. How do we coordinate our efforts as a national entity, without sacrificing or diminishing the integrity and mission of the various groups we represent and originate from? How should we approach opportunities for funding in relationship to building the urban peace and justice movement? What should be the process and protocol for dealing with the media outside of the summit experience? How should the various tasks, duties and responsibilities associated with managing the NCUPJ be assigned? Who's accountable to whom and how do we hold each other accountable?

Unfortunately, by 1996 these were the types of issues and questions that appeared to stifle the organizational development and growth of our group. To make matters worse, it appeared that key people within the NCUPJ either now had other priorities or were deeply consumed with personal issues and challenges. Carl continued to speak, tour and write, but became less and less involved with the daily work of building and expanding the NCUPJ organizationally. Prince Asiel was either traveling outside the country frequently or had left the United States altogether for sanctuary in another country (Ethiopia, Israel). We had a national office in Pittsburgh that received no financial support and very little moral or political support from other members of the National Council.

Through the advocacy and work of the local Gang Peace Council affiliate, the idea, image and legacy of the National Council was being kept alive. By then, the GPC had managed to maintain a regular office, paid and volunteer staff and various programs and projects. We also had a board composed of Sisters and Brothers who were deeply committed to the urban peace and justice movement. We were actually operating and managing two organizations with little or no support from one of them (NCUPJ), although the principles were the same.

I discussed this situation with Carl and all others who were available and willing to listen. I also believe that by now, Carl was somewhat weary from rumors and petty innuendo regarding his leadership style and personal life. He had a wife and family and was passionately committed to their well-being. In any event, we agreed that it would be better to completely integrate both organizations into the official NCUPJ.

So, later during 1996, I called for a special board meeting of GPC. After discussing and reviewing the situation, we decided to dissolve the Gang Peace Council and reincorporate it as the official National Council for Urban Peace and Justice. This transition also required the

dissolution and deactivation of the NCUPJ that was originally incorporated by myself and Carl Upchurch. Both organizations had been registered with and incorporated within the state of Pennsylvania. We now had one central organization in Pittsburgh that was <u>functionally</u>, <u>structurally</u> and <u>legally</u> equipped to coordinate the affairs of the National

Council for Urban Peace and Justice (NCUPJ) locally and nationally.

CHAPTER 10

THE MILLION MAN MARCH LOCAL MOBILIZATION COMMITTEE AND THE MILLION MAN MARCH:

We were very excited when we heard about Minister Farrakhan calling for a million man march. Black Nationalist and radical forces had all types of ideas as to what such a march might entail. Some thought perhaps a militant march on the seat of power within the United States government in demand of self-determination for Blacks in America. Others envisioned some sort of massive town hall meeting with national political figures and representatives, in which Black people would adamantly demand more progressive policy initiatives regarding jobs, economic development, police brutality; and remedies to impede and curtail the pervasive drug and gang related violence we were experiencing or witnessing every day.

Within the urban peace and justice movement, we saw the call for the march and the ensuing energy and passion behind it as an opportunity to further educate and organize our youth away from the destructive and counter revolutionary forces of street life. We saw the march as perhaps the continuation of the Black radical and revolutionary tradition of using mass mobilization as a spark or prelude to developing a grassroots movement for Black/New Afrikan freedom. After all, Ben Chavis had recently launched the National African American Leadership Summit (NAALS) in an effort to create a more robust and activist coalition for advancing a Black liberation agenda.

Chavis had been forced out of the NAACP because of political and strategic differences. Now, he would no longer be bound by the restrictive terms of his former employer (NAACP). Farrakhan and Chavis appeared to have forged a principled relationship, with the NOI and the NAALS sharing responsibility for organizing, facilitating and managing the march.

The urban peace and justice movement overwhelmingly and enthusiastically supported Minister Farrakhan's call. We wanted to reciprocate the support he and the NOI had given our fledging movement a few years earlier. We recognized that at this particular juncture in the history of our peoples' struggle, Minister Farrakhan was one of the very few individuals who could have made such a call, and solicit a <u>serious</u> and <u>passionate</u> response.

He also set off a firestorm of reaction from traditional civil rights leadership, white-liberals and Black-liberals alike, who fell over one another denouncing the planned march only because of their supposed disagreement with Farrakhan's religious and political views. Many were also media-posturing to reassure their mostly white liberal benefactors that they were 'good Black folks' who didn't support any expression of Black Nationalism. What was the purpose? After all, hadn't America elected Bill Clinton, the so-called first 'Black' president? But among the masses of Black working-class poor, youth and aspiring professionals; Farrakhan's call for an organized gathering of a million Black men on the Washington mall struck a profoundly deep and visceral nerve. Their response was truly unexpected and unpredictable.

As the appeal and popular support for the MMM grew, many of its original Black critics reversed their positions and actively sought inclusion. Meanwhile, in the Pittsburgh region, the Nation of Islam (NOI) was calling for the creation of Local Organizing Committees in mobilizing people to get on the bus. The basic challenge to the NOI being able to fulfill this directive was simply that, during this point in its development, the NOI was not very good at community organizing and mass mobilization. Their area of expertise lay in proselytizing and recruiting people into the ranks of the NOI. I also suspect that other NOI temples/masajid throughout the country faced similar challenges. But, because of the overwhelming support from millions of Blacks/New Afrikans throughout the country (and world) for the Million Man March; community organizers of various backgrounds and levels of expertise stepped up-to-the-plate. Here in the Pittsburgh area, the Gang Peace Council joined the NOI-led local organizing committee, but we quickly realized that it needed some help and direction that was community driven and led. We created a support entity which we named the Local Mobilization Committee to provide strategic assistance in actually getting people on the bus to Washington, D.C.

Prelude to the March

The murder trial of O.J. Simpson resulted in acquittal for Simpson, but clearly exposed the racist nexus between race, gender, class and the U.S. criminal justice system. It appeared that most whites in America thought O.J. was guilty of murdering his wife, Nicole Brown Simpson, and her companion Ron Goldman. They believed it to be a 'slam-dunk' case and were completely shocked, angry and dismayed when Simpson was found not guilty. After all, he was a Black man who had allegedly killed two white people, one of them being a white woman. Never mind his celebrity status as former football great, actor and pitch-man for Hertz rent-a-car. But unlike the majority of Black men (and women) appearing before the criminal courts, O.J. had money. He had some of the best lawyers that money could buy.

On the other hand, for many Blacks/New Afrikans, there was immediate jubilation upon hearing the news of O.J.'s acquittal. Finally, a Black person had either gotten justice or beaten the system at its own game. To be clear, Simpson was not universally embraced as Black Americas favorite son. He had been castigated by some Blacks for leaving his previous wife, a Black woman; and taking on a white woman as his new wife. His television and movie portrayals were not seen as very endearing to the Black community. (I have to remind people of Simpsons' role in the 'Roots' television mini-series and his role in the film 'The Klansman' as vindication). The not guilty verdict in the O.J. Simpson case was announced on **October 3, 1995.**

On **October 12, 1995**, thirty-one (31) year old Black businessman Jonny Gammage was traveling through suburban Pittsburgh that evening when he was pulled over by white police. The contingent of cops rapidly grew to over five officers, representing three different police departments (Baldwin, Whitehall, and Brentwood). All were white males.

Gammage, a resident of Syracuse, New York, had no criminal history, no outstanding warrants: no drugs or weapons were found on him or within the vehicle he was driving. His apparent crime had been that he was a young Black man driving an expensive looking car and traveling through a predominantly white area. The car actually belonged to his cousin, Ray Seals, a football player for the Pittsburgh Steelers. In the end, Jonny Gammage was beaten and strangled to death by the police. He was in town to visit his cousin and check out the city as they made preparations to attend the Million Man March on **October 16, 1995.**

We had managed to secure agreements with a few different bus companies to provide transportation for the MMM. We anticipated a possible overflow of participants, many desiring to board the bus at the last minute. Our projections were correct. The Gang Peace Council office served as Million Man March central for the vast majority of people traveling from the Pittsburgh area. We had buses rendezvousing and boarding from our office in downtown Pittsburgh until the late night and wee hours of the morning. As soon as the regularly scheduled number of buses were all filled, we contacted other bus companies for the reserve vehicles.

Finally, we filled all buses and exhausted every transportation resource available. We had plenty of travel snacks, positive videos to watch on the bus monitors and disciplined bus captains to help resolve any emergency. We even had a few sets of 'walkie-talkies' for mobile communications. A Gang Peace Council (GPC) member, who was also a member of a Black nurses association, got a group of them to serve as volunteers for the trip. We had managed to organize and mobilize the largest contingent of people attending the Million Man March from Western Pennsylvania. We were off!

The March, Its Aftermath and Legacy:

The Million Man March was definitely unlike anything we had ever seen. Black men were pouring into the Washington, D.C. area and converging on the mall by the minute. This was a watershed moment of intergenerational mobilization and unity involving Black men and youth of all ages and backgrounds. My son Diondre and his cousin Derek were also there to participate and bear witness as part of their future historical narrative. Brothers came bearing gifts and seeking guidance, direction and wisdom. They also were on their best behavior, even among so-called sworn enemies. I witnessed rival gang members engage one another as brothers in a movement for justice: offering gifts of food and attire as assurances of non-violence and tokens of peace. All up and down the vendors section, Black people were consciously and deliberately patronizing one another. That day, Black ice was just as cold, maybe colder.

The messages by all the speakers were delivered well, some content more radical and revolutionary than others, but still relevant. The focus on **redemption was important**, but **tended to overshadow the more pressing needs** of the 1.2 million Black men (and 60,000 Black women) who attended the rally and March, as well as the millions of folks we left behind. We should have emerged from the Million Man March with at least the foundation for developing three key institutions needed for our continued survival and future development:

1. Our own **Central Bank or set of regional banks and financial cooperatives** to provide needed capital resources for small business ownership and cooperative business development:
2. An **independent political party** from which to organize and strategically deploy the use of our political capital (votes, endorsements, candidates, agendas) and break the hegemony of the Democratic Party over the Black electorate;
3. Our own security unit or **national militia**; entrusted with the task and responsibility of protecting and defending Black people.

These were some of the things many of us hoped would emerge from this large and historic gathering of Black/New Afrikan people. The National African American Leadership Summit (NAALS) under the direction of Ben Chavis did make an attempt to formulate a follow-up plan of action, but it gradually spun out of focus and existence. During the following months and years, the GPC and National Council for Urban Peace and Justice would continue to provide support and participation in the various expressions of the 'Million March' movement and National African American

Leadership Summit. We either organized or participated in the Million Woman March, the Million Youth March, NAALS events and the Millions for Reparations March (organized and sponsored by the National Coalition of Blacks for Reparations in America (N'COBRA). Some of us have also participated in various MMM anniversary marches and activities, including the most recent 20th anniversary Million Man March event of 2015.

As we headed back to Pittsburgh and southwestern Pennsylvania in the early evening of October 16, 1995, we resolved to do our best to uphold the pledges made during the Million Man March and continue the work within our homes, schools and communities. We also made a solemn pledge to get justice for Jonny E. Gammage.

CHAPTER 11

JUSTICE FOR JONNY E. GAMMAGE:

The initial media reporting concerning the death of Jonny Gammage was a disgraceful display of racist media in collusion with racist police, yet unfortunately so typical of Pittsburgh's mainstream media. Radio and television coverage was dismissive regarding the 'Black motorist' from New York. The initial newspaper article was small, tucked away in between other larger news items, apparently in the hope that it would be overlooked and quickly forgotten.

Jonny Gammage was described as someone who was stopped by police for an alleged criminal activity, got into an unprovoked fight with the police and subsequently died in the process. He was methodically being projected and portrayed as a criminal and as perhaps someone who deserved to die at the hands of the police. Because he had been identified as a resident of New York state, he was also being portrayed as an outsider who attempted to break the law in small town suburban Pittsburgh. The public was being asked and groomed to marginalize and ignore his death.

Later news accounts would insinuate that Gammage was in possession of drugs, drug paraphernalia, had a criminal record and possibly outstanding warrants as well. It was implied that the fancy car Gammage was driving was either stolen or the product of illegal drug activity. However, none of this was true. Mainstream Pittsburgh media, taking its cue from local police forces (Fraternal Order of Police representatives and their attorneys) were attempting to orchestrate a cover up in the murder of an unarmed thirty-one year old Black man by a group of white suburban police.

Football is a really big deal throughout southwestern Pennsylvania. Families groom young children with any semblance of talent and football grit to get on the field. Parents and coaches delight in the prospect of producing talented players who are able to play competitively on a high school and/or college level. The goal being one day to play professional football, acquire fortune and fame and hopefully enjoy a substantially better quality of life. There's also the expectation that if successful, the homegrown athletes will make contributions of money, celebrity and resources to their community and alma mater.

Football is also big business, making millionaires of high-paid players and billionaires of team owners. Lucrative advertising, merchandizing, endorsement and broadcast contracts generate tons of money. It creates well paid jobs for coaches, trainers, apparel manufacturers, agents, attorneys, sportscasters, recruiters and well connected writers. One of the key ingredients to the success of the National Football League (NFL) has been managing its image, representation and reputation.

The highest expression and manifestation of professional football success in southwest Pennsylvania are the Pittsburgh Steelers. By October of 1995, the Steelers had amassed four super bowls, the most successful coach-quarterback tandem in super bowl history (Noll-Bradshaw): numerous playoff victories, and a constant stream of former players who were either pro-football Hall of Fame candidates or inductees. People loved the Steelers. What a shock and surprise to find out that the young Black man who died at the hands of the police was not a criminal or drug-dealer, but actually a businessman from upstate New York who was the cousin of Pittsburgh Steeler Ray Seals. He was driving his cousins' car when he was pulled over by the police. Suddenly, there was a media scramble to adjust Gammages' portrayal and history. Welcome to Steeler Country..,

Five police officers were involved in the murder of Jonny Gammage:

- Officer John Vojtas: (Brentwood Police Department)
- Lt. Milton Mulholland (Brentwood Police Department)
- Sgt. Keith Henderson: (Whitehall Police Department)
- Officer Shawn Patterson: (Whitehall Police Department)
- Michael Albert: (Baldwin Police Department)

One of those officers, John Vojtas had been implicated and later (1999) found liable in civil court for the death of his fiancée Judith Barrett. Ms. Barrett died in 1993 from a gunshot wound that came from the service revolver of Vojtas, who it was determined by the courts, had a history of abusive behavior toward Ms. Barrett. On and off the police force, he had a reputation as volatile, reactionary and violent. It's no mistake that he was specifically requested by Lt. Mulholland to intervene in the stop of Jonny Gammage.

Dismissals, Trials and Not-Guilty Verdicts:

Although a coroners' jury recommended that all five officers be charged with homicide in the death of Jonny Gammage, Allegheny County District Attorney Bob Colville (recall the 1992 Duwayne Dixon case) ignored their recommendation and charged only three of the five cops involved. All three were charged with involuntary manslaughter. In addition, Mulholland and Vojtas were charged with 3rd degree murder and official oppression.

During preliminary trial proceedings, Judge James McGregor dismissed all 3rd degree murder and official oppression charges against Mulholland and Vojtas, thereby allowing all cops to only be charged with the **misdemeanor charge** of involuntary manslaughter. By now, it's obvious that the fix is in. After highly selective and questionable processes of jury selection and two mistrials, **none** of the police officers (pigs) involved in the beating and strangulation of Jonny E. Gammage were ever convicted.

In 1998, the Gammage family agreed to a settlement of 1.5 million dollars in the death of their son. This was the result of a federal law suit filed against the boroughs of Brentwood, Baldwin, Whitehall and the cops involved in killing Jonny Gammage.

In 1999, the United States Justice Department declined to file charges in the murder of Jonny Gammage.

The Pittsburgh Steelers made the playoffs in 1995, won the AFC Championship and were poised to win their fifth (5th) championship at Super Bowl XXX. At that point in team history, the Steelers had an undefeated (4-0) Super Bowl record. However, in Super Bowl XXX, the Pittsburgh Steelers lost to the Dallas Cowboys 27-17.

The Politics of Protest: Mis-leadership and Opportunism

Holding true to our pledge, the Million Man March Local Mobilization Committee set about the struggle to get justice for Jonny Gammage. We were the first to call for and organize a series of direct protest in pursuit of justice. The first of those protest and demonstrations occurred in front of the Brentwood Municipal Building. More and more folks joined in as resident onlookers, mostly white, appeared somewhat embarrassed and angry. A few faces I actually recognized as non-profit social service providers who resented their municipality being portrayed as a haven for racist and murderous cops. Other residents weren't so conscientious: they called us names and shouted all types of vindictive slurs, even suggesting that the death of Jonny Gammage was payback for the O.J. Simpson verdict!

The Local Mobilization Committee also organized demonstrations in downtown Pittsburgh at the city-county building and courthouse. We even staged demonstrations throughout the hallways and outside of the District Attorneys' office. Other forces eventually got involved such as an organization led by Pete Schell, from Carnegie Mellon University, community activist Dorothy Urquhart and Tim Stevens of the NAACP. At some point, individuals and groups began to jockey for media attention and community support instead of focusing on pursuing justice for Jonny Gammage and his family. Some went further by attempting to isolate other groups and smear their reputation in order to gain favor with the Gammage family and their attorney.

On one occasion, I was 'summoned' to a meeting at the Hill House called by a group of local civil rights leaders who were concerned about the previous and anticipated activities of the Local Mobilization Committee regarding the murder of Jonny Gammage. I believe this happened just after we had called for a series of protest in front of District Attorney Colville's' office. I believe Brother Abdullah accompanied me at this meeting. When we arrived, we were greeted formally and those facilitating the discussion appeared to have a predetermined agenda. We listened attentively, remained respectful, but made it perfectly clear that they had no authority whatsoever to dictate the activities (strategic or tactical) of the Local Mobilization Committee, nor the Gang Peace Council (GPC). We invited them to join the Local Mobilization Committee and left in peace.

Later on, through the grapevine, we began to hear that certain area leaders were telling the Gammage family not to recognize or interact with any people from the Local Mobilization Committee, especially me. We were being portrayed as thugs, militants, and God-less people. There was an insinuation that we were trying to shake-down the family for money. Nothing could be further from the truth. The Gammage family was going through a momentous and tragic experience in dealing with the death of their son and relative. We were there to help them in the pursuit of justice. Period. To this day, I have never contacted nor spoke to any known members of the Gammage family. We have never sought any personal recognition from them whatsoever and most certainly have never had any discussions with them or their attorneys about money.

Then and now, most protest politics in the Pittsburgh region is directly or indirectly controlled by a select circle and network of civil rights leaders, politicians, unions, non-profits and foundations. They basically set the tone and agenda for what is acceptable versus unacceptable. All protest politics concerning issues and challenges in which Blacks/New Afrikans are disproportionately impacted come under the purview of the Democratic Party establishment. That includes its contingent of white and Black liberals/'progressives' too. They need and control the Black vote. As such, their collective and systemic reaction to any grassroots and genuine movement or organization is to either destroy or co-opt it. Now, as in 1995, their goal is to stay in power by fostering and maintaining Black dependency, not birthing or supporting Black freedom and self-determination.

Jerry Jackson, Jonny Gammage and the Creation of a Citizens Police Review Board:

Earlier that year, on April 6, 1995, there was another controversial police involved shooting of a Black man. His name was Jerry Jackson, who was basically executed by City of Pittsburgh police. Unlike Jonny Gammage, Jackson did indeed have a criminal history and was a formerly incarcerated person. He was trying to avoid capture by the police in a vehicle that may have been stolen. Pittsburgh police executed him within the Armstrong Tunnel and then proceeded to attempt to cover it up by claiming that Jackson turned his car around and drove toward the officers, which prompted them to fire into the vehicle in self-defense. Later, this was proven demonstrably to be a lie and attempted cover up. Police fired 51 shots into Jacksons' car, hitting him 14 times.

Eventually, a Pittsburgh Housing Authority cop, John Charmo pled guilty to involuntary manslaughter and was sentenced to eleven and a half to twenty-three months. The murder of Jerry Jackson was additional fuel for demanding the creation of a citizens police review board. However, the proposed bill was not for Allegheny County, but the City of Pittsburgh. In 1997 it became a referendum or ballot issue, in which over 57% of those voting supported it. That year, the City of Pittsburgh also agreed to a consent decree with the U.S. Justice Department regarding allegations and findings of civil rights violations.

Chapter 12

The October 22nd Coalition:

Sometime during the late nineties, around 1996 or 1997, we (GPC/NCUPJ) became aware of an organization called the **'October 22 Coalition to Stop Police Brutality, Repression and the Criminalization of a Generation'** or the October 22 Coalition for short. I'm not sure, but Wallace 'Gator' Bradley may have been the one to forward the information and invitation to our office. I think, at that time, he was a member of the October 22nds' National Coordinating Committee.

For many people involved in exposing and confronting the abuses of police authority and power, especially the police killing of civilians; the October 22 Coalition provided an extremely powerful platform. Before the advent of super cell phone technologies, the Movement for Black Lives (M4BL) and social media juggernauts such as Facebook and Instagram, communicating and documenting information regarding police abuse could be tedious, fragmented and slow. Incidents of police brutality and murder were often portrayed as isolated occurrences with little, if any systemic relationship. The people, especially victims, knew that to be untrue, but because of time and distance, validation was difficult.

The October 22 Coalition connected the victims to the perpetrators and connected the various cities, counties and states to one another. But, most importantly, the October 22 Coalition connected family, friends, survivors and activists to each other. A major component in uniting people was an initiative of the coalition titled the 'Stolen Lives Project'. The Stolen Lives Project profiled the hundreds of people who were murdered by police in various cities, counties and states throughout the United States. A powerful mobilizing and organizing tool, the Stolen Lives Project featured the photos, histories, families, friends and circumstances of death surrounding each person. And, often the failure of the criminal justice system to either charge or successfully prosecute those police involved. It clearly demonstrates the fallacy of the 'isolated incident' or 'a few rotten apples' narrative often presented by police officials, public officials and police unions as an excuse for incidents of police misconduct and murder. Another key component of the October 22 Coalition are several rallies and demonstrations held on October 22nd of every year labeled the "National Day of Protest against Police Brutality...," The National Day of Protest are organized and coordinated to be observed in multiple cities throughout the country. It is truly a powerful display of community-based, grassroots mobilization.

Sometime in 1996, in response to an invitation to take part in a national gathering scheduled in New York, myself and Kwame Scott made the trip. The conference was being held at Hunter College, in Brooklyn, and we were told that relatively inexpensive hotels or motels would be available. The 'inexpensive hotel', that we were steered to was indeed inexpensive, but not the type of place that either Kwame or I would feel comfortable spending the night in. We didn't come armed.

Fortunately, for us, one of the conference organizers and co-founders of the coalition, Carl Dix, intervened and suggested we stay the weekend at his home. We gladly accepted. Carl Dix is a co-founder and long-time member of the Revolutionary Communist Party (RCP). He also serves as one of its spokesman and representatives. He has developed a reputation for being stubborn and tenacious in his call for revolutionary struggle, but he backs it up with a dedicated work ethic as activist and organizer.

The conference itself was an eye opener. Besides anecdotal reports and alternative news reporting, it bore living proof to the pervasiveness and systemic murder of civilians by police forces across the United States. This problem and pattern wasn't just a problem for Black and Brown people; it was a problem for all people. Police in America have murdered, maimed and terrorized thousands of civilians under the guise of law and order. People of various religious or faith backgrounds, various races and ethnicities: various sexual orientations and even various classes. I came face-to-face with the fact that yes, police do kill disproportionate numbers of Black and Brown people: but they murder white folks too, and not just poor or working class white folks. They (police within the U.S.) will literally brutalize and/or murder anyone they feel is questioning their authority or right to terrorize the public.

I also came face-to-face with the surviving families of these wide-spread and systemic encounters: grieving, but courageous mothers, fathers: spouses and children from every region of the United States that represented every imaginable demographic. All were connected by the experience of losing a loved one to police brutality and murder. And, in addition, being subjected to the humiliating and gut-wrenching process of watching those responsible for their loved ones' death, not be held accountable! We gave voice and perspective to the atrocities that had occurred in the Pittsburgh region, most notably the police murders of Jerry Jackson and Jonny Gammage. They too, would now be officially included as part of the Stolen Lives Project. They too, would now be recognized and their names recited by a million voices throughout the country demanding justice for the victims and families of police terror and murder. The October 22nd Coalition and the National Day of Protest against Police Brutality were instituted in Pittsburgh after our return. Over the years, other groups, organizations and individuals such as Celeste Taylor, Kenneth Miller and Brandi Fisher have assumed leadership and kept the torch lit.

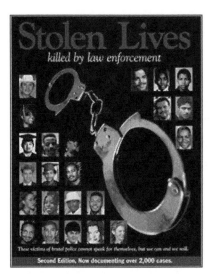

CHAPTER 13

JERICHO '98

How do I define <u>Political Prisoners</u>?

1. As people who are arrested, detained and/or incarcerated because of their political beliefs, activism and/or affiliations.
2. People who engage in armed activism and armed resistance in response to oppression and injustice resulting in their capture and incarceration are political prisoners and prisoners of war.
3. People who develop political beliefs while incarcerated and act on those beliefs in such a manner which results in them being targeted for increased surveillance, solitary confinement, additional prison time and/or state violence are also political prisoners. If they engage in purposeful armed resistance to carceral state violence and oppression, they are also prisoners of war.

<u>Prisoners of War (POWs')</u> are subject to certain protections under the agreements of the Geneva Convention. Originally the conventions were constructed and agreed upon regarding international conflicts such as World Wars I & II. The most appropriate and applicable would be the 1949 conventions and protocols (and those that follow) defining the treatment of people involved in an armed national or regional conflict such as the Black/New Afrikan liberation movement within the United States.

Despite government denial, there are scores of political prisoners and unofficial prisoners of war in the United States: for example, the numerous members of the Black Panther Party and Black Liberation Army who have been incarcerated for decades, many since the 1970's and 1980's; Leonard Peltier of the American Indian Movement (AIM), Puerto Rican freedom fighters, Anti-Imperialist activists such as David Gilbert, members of MOVE and more recently, animal rights activists, environmental justice activists and the numerous incarcerated Muslims scattered throughout the federal prison system and those under direct military lock-down in Guantanamo Bay in response to the so-called 'War on Terror'.

Many political prisoners are incarcerated in Pennsylvania. For example: members of MOVE, Mumia Abu Jamal, and the Philly Five (including Russell 'Maroon' Shoatz): Joseph Bowen, Arthur 'Cetawayo' Johnson and many politicized prisoners throughout the numerous state and federal prisons.

Because incarceration has been utilized by the U.S. ruling class as an unofficial method for controlling and containing potentially dissident and rebellious populations (e.g., Blacks), in the very broad sense, all incarcerated persons of said group could be technically labeled as political prisoners.

The purpose of Jericho 98:

The movement to free Political Prisoners and Prisoners of War was initiated through a series of communications and visits involving political prisoner/pow Jalil Mutaqim, former member of the Black Panther Party/Black Liberation Army; Safiya Bukhari, also former Panther/BLA (and former political prisoner/pow) and Herman Ferguson, longtime activist and member of the Republic of New Afrika.

The purpose of Jericho '98 is succinctly described on the Jericho Movement website: "**Jericho98** was the collective work of over 50 organizations, defense committees and groups, 64 Jericho Organizing Committees and Students for Jericho, making the issue of Recognition and Amnesty for U.S.-held political prisoners and prisoners of war a national one with its successful demonstration and rally at the White House". (https://www.thejerichomovement.com/home)

The role played by NCUPJ:

We joined with others in organizing and sponsoring a car, van and bus caravan to Jericho '98, which was held in front of the White House. Thousands of people from around the country gathered to march and rally in Washington, D.C. demanding recognition and amnesty for all political prisoners and prisoners of war. March and rally participants represented groups and individuals from various political persuasions and tendencies , all of whom were there to advocate on behalf of their comrades and all other similarly situated political prisoners and prisoners of war. I was able to reconnect with some old friends and comrades of mine that I hadn't seen in many years. There were others I had heard of from the past, but were meeting for the first time.

Networking with other groups, individuals:

Jericho provided us with an opportunity to network and build with other formations from around the country concerning the issue and work of acquiring freedom for political prisoners and POW's. Eventually, we were able to help facilitate the development of a Jericho committee in Pittsburgh, led by former political prisoner/pow Kareem Howard. We hosted Pam Africa, Safiya Bukhari and other activists who provided informational and organizing sessions to people in the Pittsburgh region. In March of 2001, the NCUPJ sponsored a Jericho Organizing Conference in Pittsburgh, featuring Safiya Bukhari and Paulette d'Auteil.

Community engagement and educating the youth:

Jericho '98 and the corresponding movement also provided us with an opportunity to educate the community, particularly the youth, about the connection between the disruption and containment of the Black liberation movement and the impact it had on our people's social and political development. It was not by accident, but rather design or systemic reaction that with the defeat and dismantling of an active and robust movement for Black/New Afrikan liberation, the national Black community was easily penetrated with the poisons of gangsterism, extreme self-indulgence, self-hatred and misogyny.

It marked a period of profound spiritual, social and political regression. Brothers and Sisters were replaced by Niggas, Bitches and Hoes. Black Liberation theology was replaced by Prosperity theology. Panthers were replaced by neighborhood drug cartels as role models of resistance to white supremacy and economic injustice. In the process, our communities have lost much of the social cohesion needed to survive, fight back and develop. Through campaigns and instrumentalities such as COINTELPRO (government created counter-intelligence program intended to identify and disrupt dissident, radical and/or revolutionary movements) and the criminal justice system, many of our best, brightest and heroic radical and revolutionary cadre were murdered, incarcerated or forced into exile.

Gradually, the potential for developing a distinct and empowering revolutionary culture was extinguished and the cultures of gangsterism and neo-colonial subservience were inserted instead. The proliferation of drug and gang related violence within our communities represents some aspect of the government successfully suppressing and dismantling the Black liberation movement of that era (circa. 1960's-early 1980's).

I applaud the numerous groups and individuals who have, throughout the years, never waned or deterred in the fight to obtain freedom for political prisoners and prisoners of war. I realize now that the demand for their freedom has to be articulated and advocated on a more local and regional basis. It has to be part of a broader and deeper movement to end mass incarceration so as to become and remain relevant to the people.

Part 3

2001-2010

- **It's About Time, BPP**
- **NAABPP**
- **Honorable Mentions**
- **Closing Comments**

Chapter 14

It's About Time, BPP

The importance of the BPP:

No other group or organization captured the imagination of Black youth in the latter half of the 20th century like the Black Panther Party. Founded by Huey P. Newton and Bobby Seale in October of 1966, the Oakland, California-based formation inspired a new generation of radicals and  revolutionaries. Much has been and continues to be written about the Black Panther Party (BPP), its ascendency, challenges and demise. Scholars and pundits alike have opined about its origin, platform, programs, leadership and the various obstacles and challenges experienced by the BPP.

Preserving its history, legacy and memorabilia:

At one point, the members, community workers and supporters of the Black Panther Party (BPP) numbered in the thousands. There were countless events, activities: rallies, marches, speeches, demonstrations: all types of communications, ranging from flyers, buttons, posters, brochures, newsletters to the famous 'Black Panther' newspaper. There were also many programs and projects, the most famous and popular being the 'Free Breakfast for

School Children', which along with other BPP initiatives served thousands of children and adults throughout the United States. The breakfast program, the free sickle cell anemia testing program among others were later incorporated and duplicated by local governments and school districts across the U.S.

In my estimation and opinion, no one individual has done more to preserve the physical, material and cultural legacy of the Black Panther Party than Billy X Jennings. He has been able to amass a huge collection of BPP memorabilia, photographs, documents, etc. that could certainly rival that of any professional curator or archivist.

Keeping us connected and inspired:

Billy X is part of 'It's About Time: BPP' which was originally formed in 1995 as an organizing committee in preparation for the 30th (1996) anniversary commemoration of the Black Panther Party. Since then it has served as a vehicle for connecting and in many ways reinvigorating former BPP members and supporters. It has continuously and consistently also served as a platform from which to educate the community, particularly the youth, concerning the actual and rich historical legacy of the Black Panther Party.

BPP 35th Anniversary Commemoration:

To that end, I was fortunate to have attended the 35th anniversary event, held in Washington, D.C. at the University of the District of Columbia in 2001. If I recall correctly, the original date for the conference was changed due to the events of 911. We had a rather large Pittsburgh contingent primarily consisting of youth from our 'Visions' rites of passage/mentoring program and accompanying NCUPJ staff. Educational workshops and numerous displays of BPP memorabilia and information made a distinct impression on all who attended. In addition, there were several former Panthers depicted in the photographs, etc. who were there to provide first-hand accounts and historical narratives. Personally, I was thrilled to see some of my former comrades from the Philadelphia chapter, notably Reggie Schell, Brown, J.T. and Stretch. I'm pretty sure Sultan ('Big Herman') was there too.

New Black Panther Party @ the BPP 35th Anniversary Commemoration:

This was also the occasion when I first had any serious conversations with representatives of the New Black Panther Party. They attended the conference and appeared to want everyone to notice their presence. We did. It became problematic when they were questioned about their attempt to revise BPP history by claiming a mythical relationship between Huey Newton and Khalid Muhammad. They actually had literature and a web-site which depicted Khalid Muhammad as a co-founder of the Black Panther Party. Bobby Seale's name and image were erased and replaced with those of Khalid Muhammad. Along with their overall demeanor, these acts produced a lot of tension. However, cooler heads prevailed. Some of us during the course of the gathering were still coming to grips with the contradictions and anguish from two decades ago resulting from the Black Panther Party 'split'.

Later, during the evening after most activities had ended, I approached NBPP leaders Malik Zulu Shabazz and Hashim Nzinga. At the time they were Chairman and Minister of Defense, respectively. I had briefly met Malik Zulu Shabazz a few years before at Jericho '98. At the time, he and a group of young activists were attempting to negotiate some space at the microphone in order to address the crowd. They expressed their frustration with some of the 'elders' who, they complained, needed to 'step-back' so they (Shabazz, et al) could speak. Upon hearing the conversation, I politely reminded him and others that this was a rally and march concerning political prisoners and prisoners-of-war and that the people that they're suggesting 'step-back' actually spent years and decades in prison. They had earned a right to speak.

However, that evening at the BPP anniversary, we had a really long and deep conversation about the history and legacy of the Black Panther Party; what it means to all in attendance that weekend, particularly those who had made so many sacrifices and experienced much collective and personal suffering during the process. We also talked about the state of affairs within Black America in general and which direction we should be headed in. In the wee hours of the morning, we embraced one another in peace and went our separate ways. Tomorrow was already upon us.

(35th anniversary photo courtesy of It's About Time, BPP)

CHAPTER 15

The National Alumni Association of the Black Panther Party (NAABPP)

Sharing some of the same directives as It's About Time: BPP, the National Alumni Association of the Black Panther Party, hereto referred to as the NAABPP for short, is likewise committed to preserving the legacy of the Black Panther Party.

Purpose:

It describes itself as such: "The purpose of the National Alumni Association of the Black Panther Party (NAABPP) is to promote and sustain the legacy of the Black Panther Party, to provide information, resources and linkages to advance and promote community organizing, to support social and criminal justice, youth development, education initiatives, advocacy and programs. The NAABPP will create resource development strategies to support ongoing and future programs and projects; and to contribute to advancing the work and support of incarcerated individuals and affected families".

Membership Organization:

A membership-based and membership-driven organization, it provides opportunities for people to network, share information, develop and coordinate programs, projects and activities that correspond with and exemplify the legacy of the Black Panther Party. The annual membership meetings and reunions have become an institution over the last several years and are held in various cities across the country. Along with a web-site, social media following and newsletter, the NAABPP provides timely information regarding the status of political prisoners/prisoners-of-world: various community and national struggles in addition to international news and perspectives. It also helps to raise awareness and/or financial support for former Panthers who face health problems and/or those who have transitioned (died).

I was very fortunate to have connected with both these organizations (It's About Time: BPP and the NAABPP) when I did. It was a reinvigoration and reconnection of sorts. A reminder and reinforcement of the protracted nature of movement building and revolutionary struggle. I only regret that at this time, I am unable to offer more than just my endorsement or membership.

Occasionally, I have an opportunity to speak with youth concerning the Civil Rights, Black Power and Black Liberation movements. When questioned about what organization or group they would have joined had they lived back then, the vast majority select the Black Panther Party.

CHAPTER 16

Honorable Mentions:

There are a number of groups, organizations and initiatives of which I had some degree or level of involvement with during this time period that are not mentioned or detailed in this book. But I would be remiss if I failed to mention a select few:

Homewood No-Dope Coalition: (1982-1984) In the early '80's Pittsburgh had developed a reputation for tolerating 'open air' drug markets. These were areas where people would congregate and openly and casually exchange drugs and money. Three well known spots in Pittsburgh were Federal Street on the Northside: Centre Avenue & Kirkpatrick in the Hill District, and Tioga and Rosedale Avenue in Homewood. Some Homewood community residents responded by organizing a broad-based neighborhood coalition to tackle the problem.

Harambee II/The Black Arts Festival: (???-1992) Over the course of a few years, Harambee developed into the premier Black arts festival of southwestern Pennsylvania, attracting visitors and vendors from as far away as Atlanta to the south and Canada to the north. Held in the Homewood community, for many years it attracted thousands of Blacks from throughout the region. Activists and community organizers such as Gail Austin, Fred Logan, Sabira Bushra and Aisha White were the chief organizers. I served on the organizing committee and helped in any way I was asked. Interest in attending and participating in Harambee began to decline as gang and drug related violence started to escalate and take hold of the Pittsburgh area. People no longer felt safe attending the event, especially if it were held in Homewood.

Advocates for African American Students in the Pittsburgh Public Schools: (circa, mid 1980's-2006) This was a dynamic advocacy group initiated by educator and activist Dr. Barbara Sizemore to address the academic achievement gap between Black and white students within Pittsburgh public schools. Also highlighted the differences in how discipline (suspension) was administered, exclusion of Black students from certain academic programs, etc.

The advocates also cited the hiring practices of the Pittsburgh district in selecting a white candidate as district Superintendent over a Black candidate who, based on both experience and education, was better qualified.

Eventually, the totality of these issues prompted the Advocates to file a 1992 lawsuit which resulted in a 2006 settlement agreement between the Advocates and the Pittsburgh school district. The agreement called for the creation of an Equity Advisory Panel to monitor district compliance in addressing the almost one-hundred (100) issues of concern. Key organizers and plaintiffs in the law suit were: Barbara Sizemore, Wanda Henderson, Huberta Jackson-Lowman, Bill Lowman, Leroy Hodge, Tamanika Howze, Kim Jackson-Morris: Anthony Mitchell, Mark Brentley, Carl Redwood, myself and many others.

I recall the several evenings of organized sit- ins and sleep-ins that took place in front of the Pittsburgh school districts' administration building. Mark Brentley would sometimes spend the night, sleeping on a cot, passing out literature and talking to anyone who would listen for as long as he could. I, on the other hand, would hang with him until the last bus back to the Northside! Mark would eventually go on to serve as a member of the Pittsburgh School Board for several years.

The student population within the Pittsburgh school district has been in decline for several years now. During the period in which the Advocates first started, there were approximately 55,000 students district wide, the majority were Black. Today, those numbers are about half of that. Economic downturns, racism, white and Black flight from public schools and gentrification have all impacted these numbers. Black families, and therefore Black children, continue to be confronted with a multitude of 'quality of life' challenges that impact student performance. These challenges include poverty, under-employment, unemployment, homelessness, substance abuse, violence and the impact of mass incarceration.

The issue of poor school performance and reducing or eliminating the academic achievement gap between Black and white students is symptomatic of the much larger and profound problem of white-supremacy and economic injustice (capitalism). Until we collectively come to terms with this and prioritize the dismantling of white-supremacy and predatory capitalism (and all that comes along with it), we will continue, to quote Dr. Barbara Sizemore: "Walk in circles".

Chapter 17

Closing Comments:

Revolution is a process, not an event or isolated series of events. It requires patience, courage, tenacity, perspective and most importantly faith. No matter how passionate or strategic or militant we may be or think that we are; the willingness to take on the empire of white-supremacy and economic injustice requires a tremendous amount of faith.

Faith, that in our lifetime or during the lifetime of our children and grandchildren, the monster will be defeated and brought to its knees. No doubt, that must have been the type of faith our ancestors developed and maintained all throughout the experiences of capture, enslavement, resistance, Jim Crow and the periods of the Nixon-Reagan-Clinton counter-revolution of '69-'92.

Now in this new period of resurgent radicalism, the militant pursuit of social justice and the growth of revolutionary ideation; we must draw lessons and inspiration from our past, even the most recent past. I hope these memoirs are able to contribute to this process. May Allah strengthen our will and resolution toward victory in our lifetime and the lifetimes of those that follow. Ameen.

Made in the USA
Middletown, DE
17 June 2019